Harvey K. Littleton
A Retrospective Exhibition

Essay by Joan Falconer Byrd

High Museum of Art   Atlanta 1984

Exhibition Schedule

Renwick Gallery
National Museum of American Art
Smithsonian Institution, Washington, D.C.
March 30 — September 3, 1984

American Craft Museum II
New York City
November 16, 1984 — January 12, 1985

Brunnier Gallery and Museum
Iowa State University, Ames, Iowa
February 10 — April 7, 1985

High Museum of Art
Atlanta, Georgia
April 28 — June 16, 1985

Milwaukee Art Museum
Milwaukee, Wisconsin
September 15 — October 30, 1985

Portland Museum of Art
Portland, Maine
November 20, 1985 — January 5, 1986

Cover Photograph: 98. Yellow Crown, 1983

Edited by Kelly Morris
Designed by Jim Zambounis

Library of Congress Catalogue No. 84-80145
ISBN 0-939802-20-1

This exhibition is supported in part by a grant from
the National Endowment for the Arts, a Federal agency.

Foreword

The emergence of the artist/craftsman, a recent if not new state of affairs, has interesting and positive implications, both in an economic and in a cultural sense. Harmonious traditions shared by artists and craftsmen which had developed over centuries of collaboration came to an end in post-revolutionary 19th century Europe. Industrialization nearly put the makers of furniture and textiles and of ceramic, glass, and metal objects out of business, and the disappearance of artists' guilds placed the painters and sculptors in a precarious if somewhat romanticized isolation from which they have yet to escape.

A profound reaction to the materialism of the industrial age led to the establishment of certain craftsmen's workshops even before the turn of the century. This in turn has fostered a new attitude in recent years among artists and makers of traditional utilitarian objects which has begun to obscure the lines of distinction between their creative activities. Sculpture has become almost flat and painting three-dimensional, furniture is not necessarily functional, and the traditional crafts objects assume decorative, pictorial, and even narrative qualities, while textiles have become sculpture.

When Harvey Littleton turned to glass as an expressive medium two decades ago, his principal preoccupation was with technique; but there is no question that he saw his contribution as that of a sculptor, as that of an artist rather than simply a craftsman. It is significant that his first work in glass had the most ancient of all artistic themes, the female figure. Littleton's course of development since the early 1960s is vividly described in Joan Falconer Byrd's catalogue essay. Ms. Byrd, herself a student of Littleton's, is also responsible for the notes on form and the chronology of the artist's career. Her sister, Mary Byrd Davis, compiled the bibliography.

Harvey Littleton's work has been as an artist, as a researcher, as a teacher and lecturer, and as the head of a rather expansive operation which involves a number of interns, assistants, and visiting artists who, besides making glass, record, photograph, pack, and transport the glass objects which emerge from Littleton's studio in a steady progress. Several of Littleton's family members are involved full-time in the enterprise and have been instrumental in the organization of this exhibition. I must thank, especially, his wife Bess for providing much information (and her most agreeable hospitality), his daughter Maurine for compiling the catalogue information, his son John for many of the photographs of his father's works, and his son Tom for taking charge of the intricacies of packing the exhibition and transporting it to each of the participating museums.

Our appreciation is extended to my colleagues Lloyd Herman, Paul Smith, Lynette Pohlman, Gerald Nordland, and John Holverson for inviting this exhibition to be shown in their respective institutions. On the High Museum's part, I acknowledge the good work of our editor, Kelly Morris, and designer Jim Zambounis, who were responsible for the production of this catalogue. Our sincerest thanks are extended to the lenders to this exhibition and to the National Endowment for the Arts for their grant toward this project.

Above all, I wish to pay tribute to Harvey Littleton for his seminal work as a glass sculptor and his keen interest in our efforts to bring together a representation of his life's work. His participation was crucial to the project.

Gudmund Vigtel
Director
High Museum of Art

Harvey Littleton and Studio Glass

Joan Falconer Byrd

The development of Harvey K. Littleton as an artist is intertwined with the history of the studio glass movement in the United States. In its early stages the movement itself was largely his creation and, until recently, his reputation as studio glass pioneer has perhaps overshadowed his art. Littleton's early work involved broad experimentation, and since leaving university teaching seven years ago to focus on creating the body of work which he regards as his *raison d'être,* he has steadily built on his early investigations. This long development culminates in Littleton's current series of sculptures. Considerable in scale and instinct with energy, the sculpture expresses the artist's unabated excitement at working in the medium which he pioneered in contemporary art.

From the vantage point of twenty years of the American studio glass movement, it is obvious that Littleton was tutored for his founding role long before the dream began to take shape. Born in 1922 in the factory town of Corning, New York, where his father, Jesse Littleton, was director of research for Corning Glass Works, the artist was exposed to science and industry at an early age. He remembers that his father, a pioneering physicist and the originator of Pyrex cookware, could never eat jello at dinner without pulling apart the dessert with a spoon and thoughtfully watching the cracks assume the shape of breakage lines in glass. The artist's own fascination with glass began when he went with his father to the laboratory on Saturdays. The boy was enchanted by the patterns and rainbow colors revealed in pieces of crystal held under the polariscope.

Although art glass was out of favor during the Depression and neither of his parents was interested in glass as an art medium, Littleton was aware of Frederick Carder, founder and art director of Steuben Glass, who lived nearby in a house with a lovely pear tree that hung invitingly over the alley on the way to the candy store. Many years later, when his interest focused on glass, Littleton came to admire Carder as a fighter and a rebel; but as he grew into his teens, he knew Carder only as a prominent local figure and long-standing member of the board of education. Carder was responsible for including in the design of the Corning Free Academy a very large art room with a north skylight, where Littleton studied throughout his high school years. In extension classes offered there by nearby Elmira College, Littleton received the foundations of a neo-classic art training typical of the period before World War II. He studied the academic disciplines of figure drawing and modeling under sculptor Enfred Anderson. Years later, when he was director of the Arnot Art Gallery in Elmira, New York,

Anderson was to purchase the first work Littleton ever exhibited: a neo-classic torso cast in glass (no. 2).

In 1939 Littleton gamely attempted to uphold a family tradition by enrolling in the University of Michigan as a physics major, but within two years he had found these studies to be less than compelling and had transferred to the Cranbrook Academy of Art in Bloomfield Hills, Michigan. At Cranbrook he studied sculpture with Marshall Fredericks. Again the course involved modeling the figure in clay, making a mold, and casting the piece in plaster, after which it was painted in imitation of bronze—a procedure which contrasted sharply with the principle of direct involvement in the material which would underlie the studio glass movement.

While he was at Cranbrook, Littleton worked as assistant in the studio of the prominent Swedish-American sculptor Carl Milles. Near the end of his semester at the school, the student made a formal appointment with Milles to discuss the prospects of supporting himself as a sculptor. Understandably daunted by Milles's comment that "he knew a very fine policeman in Brussels who was an excellent sculptor," Littleton made a compromise with his parents: he returned to the University of Michigan in the fall of 1941 to study industrial design.

In the meantime, Littleton's familiarity with glass deepened as he worked in different areas of the Corning Glass plant during summer vacations. In 1941 he was employed as inspector of handblown cookware, becoming fascinated with the sensuous beauty of the blowing process even as he developed a taste for smashing the forms that failed to meet plant standards. The following summer he was a mold maker for the Vycor Multiform project laboratory and was thus involved with a process similar to that of *pâte-de-verre*. It was in the white, almost opaque Multiform material that he executed his first work in glass, making a casting in 1942 of an academic torso he had modeled in clay (no. 1).

Service in the Army Signal Corps sent him overseas for almost three years, during which he was assigned the responsibility of maintaining an encoding device. Littleton and a corpsman assigned to teletype maintenance collaborated in developing a mechanical method of automatically decoding the messages transmitted by teletype tape. Awarded a commendation for this work, Littleton chose to spend his final months in service, following the close of World War II, at the Brighton School of Art in England. Once again he concentrated on sculpture. A small torso which he modeled from life pleased him; he had it bisque fired and carried it across the Atlantic in his duffel bag in 1945.

Discharged from the Army after spending Christmas at Fort Dix, New Jersey, Littleton took the clay torso to the laboratory in Corning, where he made a five-part piece mold and cast the sculpture in Multiform glass in January 1946 (no. 2). Excited by the transformation of the piece from earthenware into the translucent material, he experimented with a sequence of processes in refining the surface of the form: lightly abrading it, fusing it with an oxygen torch, and then dulling it again. After he returned to the University of Michigan that winter, he exhibited the piece in the *Michigan Artists' Exhibition* in Detroit; the following year the sculpture was purchased for the permanent collection of the Arnot Art Gallery in Elmira, New York. From 1946 on, Littleton showed his work widely and continuously, but it was not until 1962 that he again exhibited glass.

With the enrollment increases produced by the G.I. Bill, college art programs nationwide received an impetus that found vigorous expression in the contemporary crafts movement. Even as a veteran, however, Littleton was not ready to make a radical break with his family in his choice of career; when he returned to the university under the G.I. Bill, he concentrated on completing his degree in industrial design. His exploration of the Multiform process had led him to the conclusion that "there ought to be on-going aesthetic experimentation in material at the Corning Glass Works apart from production," and upon his graduation he was encouraged by his father to submit a proposal to Corning for establishing a workshop within the factory for the development of new ideas. This proposal was the first of many Littleton has submitted over the years. While more recent projects involving small furnaces have met with generous approval on the part of the Corning Glass Works Foundation, the 1947 proposal did not. Littleton gave up all thought of working in glass: "I thought, as did all people in Corning, that glass was an industrial material and had to be made in a factory with a team of workers rather than in a studio working alone."

In 1947 Littleton married Bess Tamura, an art student from Hawaii whom he had met at the University of Michigan the previous year, and joined two friends in establishing a design business in Ann Arbor, Michigan. Among a variety of activities—from painting signs to designing doorknobs—the firm undertook the reproduction of photographic images on a photo-sensitive glass developed by Corning Glass Works. Before being licensed to use the process, Littleton was required to attend a training session at the factory. Instructed at the Glass Works in the method of finishing the edges of the photographic pieces, he gained his initial experience in grinding and polishing glass.

Later a commission to build several potter's wheels led Littleton into teaching ceramics, a field which he had studied in a tentative way while involved in sculpture. Gradually the teaching at the Goat's Nest Ceramics Studio proved of greater interest than the design firm, and Littleton was drawn into the growing contemporary crafts movement. Littleton's future role as an indefatigable organizer in the field was foreshadowed by his leadership at the private studio, which became a co-operative pottery, the Ann Arbor Potters' Guild, which still thrives today.

In 1949 Littleton accepted a teaching position at the Museum School of the Toledo Museum of Art in Toledo, Ohio, where he also built much of the equipment for the ceramics department. Toledo has been a center for the glass industry since the nineteenth century, and its museum boasts one of the finest collections of historical glass in the country. Littleton familiarized himself with this collection during the two years he taught at the museum. The friendship he formed at this time with Otto Wittmann, who later became director of the museum, would prove important for the development of studio glass.

While he was teaching in Toledo, Littleton returned to Cranbrook Academy, where he studied with Finnish-born constructivist potter Maija Grotell. Her uncompromising view of pottery as an art form was to have a lasting influence on the standards Littleton set for himself: "Being an artist, to her, was the ultimate. Not the level of craftsmanship or the direction of your work—functional or not—but whether you were an artist." With characteristic commitment and energy, Littleton completed his MFA degree at Cranbrook in 1951, despite an arduous schedule of commuting between Toledo and Bloomfield Hills.

That autumn, Littleton joined the faculty of the University of Wisconsin, and he and Bess settled their growing family on a farm in Verona, eight miles outside of Madison. For several years, they operated a small dairy on the land. One of the older farm buildings was converted into a pottery studio where Littleton threw, glazed, and fired functional stoneware. Well known at the craft fairs in the Chicago area, he also sold his work to galleries on a circuit from Chicago to New York City. He was invited to show his work both in this country and abroad, and regularly took part in competitive exhibitions such as the distinguished Ceramic National organized by the Syracuse Museum of Fine Arts. The pottery business and the dairy gave Littleton independence from the university, and a ceramics equipment and supply business which he started after selling the dairy herd provided the funding for his early experiments in glass.

Littleton inherited a belief in the value of university teaching from his parents, whose families had both long been involved in higher education. However, in the fifties it must have seemed unlikely that Littleton would spend a quarter of a century on the faculty of the University of Wisconsin, be appointed to a full professorship, and be chosen to serve two terms as department chairman. An ambitious young man, Littleton was by his own account "obstreperous," and he fitted but poorly into the Department of Art and Art Education he encountered upon his arrival on campus in 1951.

Involvement in the nascent American Craft Council offered him a certain strength at the university, as well as providing friendship with like-minded colleagues across the country. In 1954, together with Michael and Frances

Higgins of Chicago and other area craftsmen, he founded the Midwest Designer-Craftsmen, which later became the regional arm of the American Craft Council. The Higginses were involved in molding and enriching manufactured sheet glass, using techniques such as enameling, slumping, and lamination. A few years later, it was Michael Higgins who gave a special conviction to the challenge laid before Littleton by the American Craft Council to bring hot glass into the studio.

In the fifties Littleton completed several research projects in ceramics, the earliest of which was a study of vapor glazing, supported by the first of several grants he would receive from the university research committee. His interest in salt glazing led him to spend several weeks in 1957 working at the traditional Jugtown Pottery in the North Carolina piedmont, where he joined in the firing of the groundhog salt kiln. He was awarded university travel support later the same year for the study of Islamic influence on contemporary Spanish pottery, and he agreed to undertake a small research project for the Corning Museum of Glass while he was in Spain.

Littleton remained intrigued by the possibility of studio glass, and he asked Arthur Houghton, then president of the Steuben Glass Works, if he knew of any artists in Europe working alone in glass. Having received from Houghton the name of Jean Sala, the Littletons located the artist in his Spanish antiquities gallery in Paris. On a visit to Sala's former studio in the Montparnasse area, they were fascinated by a group of pieces made before he had stopped working in glass in 1950. Following four and a half months of work in a traditional pottery in the south of Spain, Littleton made a second discovery affecting his interest in studio glass. Taking Bess and their four children to Italy, where he had seen duty with the Signal Corps during the war, he was surprised to discover seven small glass factories in Naples. Later he spent several months visiting more than fifty glass factories on the island of Murano. Although Littleton met with a cool reception in Murano owing to the jealousy with which the glassworkers guarded their traditions and trade secrets, the experience of seeing small shops built around two-man demonstration furnaces was compelling. He became convinced for the first time that it was possible to blow glass outside the context of industry and that an artist could have a fully functional glass facility in his own studio.

His enthusiasm fired, Littleton returned to the United States. Stopping in Corning to report the results of his research in Spain to Paul Perrot, then director of the Corning Museum of Glass, he visited Frederick Carder in his office at the old Steuben factory to announce his idea of working in hot glass. Immediately upon his return to Verona, Littleton began to melt small batches of various glasses in his studio, using as a crucible one of his stoneware bowls set inside an old ceramics kiln.

In 1958 the American Craft Council attracted national attention to glass art when it presented the first major retrospective exhibition of the work of Louis Comfort Tiffany. The following year, when the Corning Museum of Glass mounted *Glass '59: A Contemporary Worldwide Survey,* the picture of international activity in the medium appeared in sharp focus. Less than ten per cent of the work was made by studio glassworkers, those pieces being fused and laminated. The overwhelming preponderance of the work, including every blown piece in the exhibition, was factory made.

When the American Craft Council organized its Third National Conference at Lake George, New York, Littleton was chosen to chair a panel on glass composed of Michael and Frances Higgins and Earl McCutcheon, artists working with preformed glass, and Paul Perrot of the Corning Museum of Glass. Recounting his experiences abroad the previous year, Littleton ventured tentative conclusions concerning the feasibility of hot glass as a medium for the artist. The response of the other panelists was a challenge to Littleton to bring his vision of studio glassblowing to reality. By the time the ACC convened its Fourth National Conference in Seattle in 1961, Littleton was ready to present a paper on his research and to support his presentation with a display of several small lumps of glass which he had melted in his studio and had afterwards cut and polished into faceted sculptures (no. 8).

Having discussed his experiments before a national forum, Littleton was not the only craftsman to seek foundation funding in the early sixties for a proposal to initiate a hot glass program. However, his requests for support were singularly modest. He remembers explaining to one administrator, "All I need is a garage." And in 1961 he found that garage, on the grounds of the Toledo Museum of

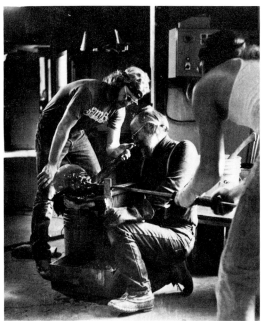

Art. Otto Wittmann, who had written several recommendations in support of Littleton's grant proposals, offered him the use of the building where the museum's lawnmowers were kept, for a one-week workshop seminar exploring hot glass. The following March, Littleton brought a small pot furnace he had built at his farm and hooked it up in the museum garage with the help of Norm Schulman, pottery instructor at the museum school. Dominick Labino, then director of research for Johns Manville Corporation and a friend of Littleton's since the artist had taught pottery at the museum, volunteered a low-melting glass formula.

The group of eight craftsmen who assembled for the workshop in March 1962 was composed primarily of potters. Littleton's longtime friends Michael and Frances Higgins were the only glassworkers. The ceramists included Karl Martz of the University of Indiana, John Stephenson of the University of Michigan, Clayton Bailey (a graduate student of Littleton's), and two former pottery students of Littleton's from Toledo. Completing the group was Tom McGlauchlin, who had received his master's degree under Littleton in 1960 and was teaching at Cornell College in Iowa. Today McGlauchlin is a prominent glass artist as well as head of the glass program at the museum school in Toledo.

The eagerly awaited first batch of glass melted during the workshop proved a disaster, owning to a faulty reading of Labino's formula. Labino himself then directed the conversion of the pot furnace into a small day tank, which he

11

supplied with the low-melting formula #475 glass marbles he had developed for the production of fiberglass. The long-working #475 glass provided an excellent melt for glassblowing, and for the remainder of the week the workshop participants experimented with the glass in shifts around the clock. On the last day of the workshop, further important assistance arrived when Harvey Leafgreen, a retired glassblower from the Libbey Glass plant in Toledo, paid an unexpected visit and stayed to give a two-hour demonstration of his craft.

The more widely advertised second Toledo workshop, held in June 1962, brought together participants of more varied backgrounds and from a broader area of the country. The diversity of students was made possible through the financial assistance of Just Lunning, president of Georg Jensen's in New York City. The two-week workshop featured a complex program in which Littleton shared teaching responsibilities with Dominick Labino, Harvey Leafgreen, and Norm Schulman, while gallery talks were given by the curatorial staff of the museum. Throughout the two Toledo workshops which he organized, Littleton himself was the most avid learner of the group. Of all involved in these historic presentations, only Littleton, Labino, and McGlauchlin have continued to do significant work with hot glass.

A trip to Europe later that summer for the purpose of surveying schools teaching hot glass proved disappointing to Littleton because he found the programs to be industrial in orientation, "with no students working directly in the material." However, he and Bess enjoyed a second visit with Jean Sala in Paris, and in Bavaria Littleton met a glass artist of his own generation who was to have a seminal influence on his career.

The impact of Littleton's encounter with the expressionistic sculpture of Erwin Eisch was enormous. Eisch worked in the factory which he and his two younger brothers had founded in 1952 when he was just twenty-five. Although Eisch worked in a factory situation, and although he blew glass with assistance—an issue which Littleton regarded as crucial in the early years of studio glass—he was a sculptor making powerful statements in hot glass. The two men began a friendship which would see them internationally acclaimed as leaders of a new movement in twentieth century art. Littleton returned to the United States, his excitement at a high pitch. He stopped off in Corning to share his enthusiasm with the grand old man Frederick Carder. This was Littleton's last visit with Carder, who died the following year at the age of one hundred.

Littleton's imagination was now wholly captured by the medium of glass. By the summer of 1962 the only pottery he was making consisted of stoneware crucibles in which he melted #475 glass marbles, although he continued to show his ceramics in invitational group exhibitions for another year. In the fall of 1962 Littleton opened his glass studio one day a week to six students in ceramics whom he taught under an independent study program. Although none of the initial group of students continued to work in glass, a young sculptor who joined the class the following semester became the first to receive an MFA degree in the new medium and became the first Wisconsin graduate to teach glassblowing. Today Marvin Lipofsky has worldwide influence and heads one of the major glass programs in the country at California College of Arts and Crafts.

In the autumn of 1963 the first hot glass program at a university in the United States gained solid footing. An anonymous grant, given through the influence of Dominick Labino, enabled Littleton to secure sufficient university funding to rent and equip an off-campus space in Madison for a student studio. After building their own furnaces and annealing ovens, the students settled down to a demanding routine of blowing glass in the new studio seven days a week.

Littleton's goal of introducing hot glass into the curriculum of the university was not fully satisfied by the initiation of the program in Madison. In the fall of 1962 and the first half of the following year, he lectured extensively at art schools and universities as well as to designer-craftsmen's organizations throughout the Midwest and the Northeast. Beginning with what he termed "a review of the past five years' struggle to develop tools and techniques and to interest someone in the project," he showed slides of his studio and exhibited pieces he had made and the tools with which he worked. The openness with which Littleton discussed his growing understanding of the technical requirements and skills of glassblowing contrasted sharply with the tradition of secrecy which he had encountered among the glassworkers of Murano. By sharing the results of his investigations of the medium, he laid the foundation for the free exchange of information that has stimulated the development of the glass movement in its first two decades.

Painstakingly teaching himself the discipline of the craft, Littleton at first focused on blowing small, symmetrical vases. His earliest one-man shows consisted exclusively of functional pieces. Invited by associate curator Vivian Scheidemantel to show his glass at the Art Institute of Chicago in the summer of 1963, he exhibited approximately sixty vases, plates, bowls, and paperweights in a single case in the Decorative Arts Department of the museum.

But Littleton was determined not to be limited by the confines of functional form in glass as he had been in pottery. The breakthrough for him came when he reconsidered a form which he had impatiently smashed in the blowing process and refused in the furnace. The broken open container forms recalled Littleton's experience of smashing glass vessels as a quality control officer at the glass factory in Corning; the persistence of the theme of breakage in his work illustrates his thesis that "an artist's experience is digested into creative energy over time."[1] This series of forms marked the beginning of Littleton's "attempt to get at the essence of material." In his exhibitions of this period functional glass pieces stood in counterpoint to experimental forms more expressive of Littleton's driving energy.

The series of shapes smashed and remelted—in flagrant denial of function—embodied a turning point not only in Littleton's career but in the history of glass as well. The pieces did not fit readily within the tradition of glass art, and yet the medium in which they were made initially barred them from consideration as sculpture. The first piece in this series belonged to the select group of works Littleton describes as "the seminal pieces, those pieces that lead you somewhere: they are the distillation of creativity." Although the piece retained the shape of the vase on which Littleton had been working when he attacked the form in vexation, the Museum of Contemporary Crafts elected not to include it in Littleton's one-man exhibition which opened in New York City in 1964. Littleton's more radical work found a champion, however, in Mildred Constantine of the Museum of Modern Art, at whose instigation the piece was purchased for the Design Collection of the museum in 1965. Associate curator of the Department of Architecture and Design, Ms. Constantine was less effective in obtaining the support of the acquisitions committee of the museum for the purchase of a later Littleton work in the same series. *Copper Gray Form* (no. 22) pushed the denial of function further: the free form was mounted with its open end attached to a marble base. The piece was rejected because it defied classification. Patently nonfunctional, the work was not considered appropriate for the Design Collection; and because it was made of glass, the Sculpture Department showed no interest in it.

The opportunity to spread the word about studio glass before an international audience came in the summer of 1964 at the two-week-long first meeting of the World Congress of Craftsmen in New York City. A trustee of the American Craft Council, which organized the event, Littleton served on the conference planning committee. Among the participants in the congress at Columbia University were glass designers from industries in the United States and abroad, who were astonished to see Littleton and his university glass students set up a small furnace built by Labino, melt a tankful of #475 marbles, and begin to blow glass. Most of the designers were amused by what they called Littleton's "do it yourself glass art." But Sybren Valkema of Holland, then designer at the Royal Leerdam Glass Factory and associate director of the Gerrit Rietveld Academy, was delighted; Littleton's demonstration facility enabled Valkema to blow glass for the first time. Valkema immediately grasped the possibilities opened up by the studio-sized furnace, and the following year he constructed the first "little furnace" in Europe when he built a similar day tank at the Rietveld Academy in Amsterdam.

Erwin Eisch, who was an invited delegate to the conference, worked at a studio-sized furnace for the first time when he joined Littleton and his class in demonstrating in New York City. The experience was apparently a revelation even to Eisch, who is remembered to have pronounced at the close of the meeting, "The little furnace is the future." Eisch traveled to Madison with Littleton at the end of the conference to share teaching responsibilities with him during a four-week summer session at the university. In the increasing complexity of Littleton's pieces in this period, culminating in the anthropomorphic forms of 1964-65 (see no. 19), the influence of the highly personal sculptures of Eisch is unmistakable.

It was in 1964 that Littleton began to see his efforts rewarded. The studio glass movement, which was beginning to have international impact, was also taking hold in widely separated areas of the United States. When Marvin Lipofsky completed his MFA degree that summer, he traveled to the West Coast, where he introduced glass to the campus of the University of California at Berkeley. Among the glass programs initiated as a result of the demonstration at the World Congress of Craftsmen were those at Haystack Mountain School of Crafts in Maine and San Jose State College in California. The very productive program at San Jose State was begun by Robert Fritz, whose enthusiasm had been so aroused by the presentation at the conference that he stopped in Madison to take part in the joint summer session taught by Littleton and Eisch before returning west.

That same year, Littleton assumed the chairmanship of the Department of Art and Art Education at the University of Wisconsin. His commitment to the academic world, combined with his proclivity for politics and his business acumen, made him a remarkably effective administrator. Littleton attacked the problems of the department with vigor and tenacity, securing a needed increase in funding for departmental activities; and the department was able to implement an artist-in-residence program during his first year as chairman. Littleton's first term as an administrator also dealt him such lively surprises as the widely publicized arrest of a group of art students who had staged a "happening" in Milwaukee in which two nude models bathed by candlelight. His first period as department chair lasted until 1967, and he was later elected to serve an additional two years.

Littleton's teaching had always been directed towards the best of his students rather than towards what he regarded as "some fictitious mean," and his hot glass program drew from a pool of energetic and intensely motivated graduate students educated in a variety of fields. Operating their own studio in Madison, the students gained the practical knowledge they needed to found new glass facilities in this country and overseas. These were the years when increased student enrollment precipitated by the Vietnam war led to rapid expansion of university art programs across the United States, and most of the students who completed Littleton's program quickly found openings in the teaching field.

A pioneering contribution was made by Sam Herman, a Littleton student who received his graduate degree from the university in 1964 and traveled to Edinburgh that autumn as a Fulbright Scholar. Although he was never able to construct a hot glass facility at the Edinburgh College of Art, Herman was later invited to become a tutor at the Royal College of Art in London, where he built England's first studio furnace. While the Royal College had previously offered a strong program in glass design, Herman involved the students in working directly with hot glass for the first time. The thriving glass community in England today owes its origin to his efforts.

Several of his students proved to be the same kind of dynamic promoters of glass as Littleton himself. Two glass artists graduated in 1967 are among the most influential alumni of the Wisconsin glass program. Dale Chihuly established the Pilchuck Glass Center in Washington state while building the glass department at the Rhode Island School of Design. The peripatetic Fritz Dreisbach, who constructed the glass facility at the Toledo Museum of Art, became one of the founders and sustaining forces behind the international Glass Art Society, gradually making Penland School of Crafts in North Carolina his center of operations.

At the close of his three years as department chairman, Littleton took a year's leave of absence from the university in order to pursue his creative work. Erwin Eisch was visiting professor at the university in November and December of that year, after which Sybren Valkema took over the teaching responsibilities in the spring. Eisch and an assistant worked in Littleton's studio for a month, making pieces for exhibition in the United States. After he returned to Frauenau, his influence on Littleton remained so strong that at one time even Bess Littleton found it impossible to distinguish between the work of the two men.

In early 1968 Littleton resolved to turn from the complexity of form characteristic of Eisch to minimal statements based on the column and the tube. Some of the columns were bent into loops by the action of gravity, and thus evolved the famous loop series which was to preoccupy the artist for more than a decade. Having begun to mount his sculptures on marble and then on metal bases several years earlier, when the glass itself was little more than an inverted vase, now Littleton frequently integrated glass tubes with machined metal forms in constructivist sculptures. Having found his stride, Littleton continued to work within a strictly simplified mode when he blew glass in the Eisch factory in Bavaria in the summer of 1968; within a month, he had completed thirty pieces for exhibition in Europe. The sculptures Littleton made in Frauenau offered a striking counterpoint to those of Eisch when the work of the two men was exhibited together in 1969, first at the Handwerkskammer in Munich and then in Cologne.

In the fall of 1969, *Objects: USA* opened at the Smithsonian Institution under the sponsorship of the S. C. Johnson Company. Organized by gallery owner Lee Nordness, the exhibition presented work in nine crafts media, including several outside the accepted areas of fiber, clay and metal. Subsequently traveling throughout the country, the show announced to the public that the crafts in the United States, which had experienced explosive growth since World War II, had attained the level of art. One of Littleton's pieces in this exhibition was *Falling Blue* (no. 29), a supple composition of blown and cut tubes of copper glass. Among the most widely known of Littleton's early sculptures, this work is now in the collection of the American Craft Museum. Of the eighteen glassblowers represented in the exhibition in addition to Littleton himself, half had studied with the artist at the University of Wisconsin; and others, taught by these Wisconsin graduates, were second generation students of his.

At the same time that *Objects: USA* was making its way to museums throughout the country, student demonstrations were wracking American university campuses. In 1969 Littleton again accepted the position of department chairman at the University of Wisconsin, holding this post during the height of the protests at Madison. Himself a rebel, he sympathized with the students even as he was deeply troubled by the violence of their demonstrations against the university. This period of protest was to mark the end of the great expansion of American university programs. By 1971 more than fifty schools, colleges, and universities offered instruction in hot glass; but from the early 1970s on, Littleton was to find it increasingly difficult to locate teaching positions for the graduates of his programs.

In 1971 Littleton's book *Glassblowing: A Search for Form* was published. As its title emphasizes, rather than focusing on technique, the book asserts Littleton's conviction that studio glassblowing must find its validity as a means of artistic expression. Reflecting the philosophy of Maija Grotell, and in keeping with Littleton's own practice as a teacher, the book is less concerned with giving answers than with inspiring the interaction between artist and material.

At the close of Littleton's second tour of duty as department chairman, he took a semester's salaried leave to renew his association with the European glassmakers. In the spring of 1972, he accepted an invitation from the factory of Val Saint-Lambert near Liège, Belgium, where the extensive facilities of the factory were put at his service. The blown, cut, and polished crystal sculptures he made at this time—and displayed in Liège the following December—show a sophistication inspired by the brilliance of the glass. Littleton returned to Europe in spring 1973 as guest artist at the Rietveld Academy in Amsterdam, after which he spent six weeks working at the Eisch factory. The sculptures made in Bavaria were later shown along with those of Eisch in a two-man exhibition at the nineteenth century Viennese glasshouse of J. & L. Lobmeyr.

Working in the cutting rooms of the Val Saint-Lambert and Eisch factories had fueled Littleton's enthusiasm for cold working processes. Feeling a need to add these capabilities to the repertory of studio glassworkers in the United States, he organized a seminar-workshop in cold working techniques which took place in his studio in Verona in the summer of 1974. Funded by grants from the National Endowment for the Arts, the Steuben Glass Works, and the Corning Glass Works Foundation, the workshop featured demonstrations of the traditional crafts of cutting and engraving by craftsmen from Corning and Steuben side by side with new sandblasting techniques. As a result of the sandblasting experiments at a local monument works, Littleton embarked on a challenging new phase of his career: printing from glass plates.

Using the products of his various demonstrations at the seminar, Littleton treated the abraded panes of window glass as intaglio plates which he inked and ran through an etching press. With the assistance of printmaker Warrington Colescott, a colleague at the university, Littleton solved the problems inherent in using glass plates. Employing sandblasting to etch areas of varied depth in the glass surface, he developed a method of printing that provided effects similar to color viscosity printing but with color qualities impossible to achieve with metal plates. It was not until eight years later that Littleton learned there was a historic precedent for this use of glass: a series of intaglio prints from glass plates were produced in mid-nineteenth century Vienna and exhibited in the Crystal Palace Exhibition in London before technical problems caused the experiments to be discontinued. By 1975 Littleton had begun to exhibit his prints along with his sculptures, and the two were presented together at the Bergstrom Art Center in Neenah, Wisconsin, in December 1975, in a retrospective exhibition which later traveled to the Charles H. MacNider Museum in Mason City, Iowa. Littleton's preoccupation with color mixing in his prints inspired a concern with similar relationships in his sculpture, and from this point on color became increasingly important in his sculptural pieces.

By 1976 museums and galleries were responding as eagerly to the glass movement as the schools and universities had done a decade earlier. The annual Glass Art Society conference that year was held in conjunction with a national exhibition of studio work at the Corning Museum of Glass. In the same year the Contemporary Art Glass Group, which had opened a gallery in New York City in 1974, sponsored a national show at Lever House in New York City, and Habatat Galleries near Detroit held its first annual nationwide glass exhibition.

In 1976 Littleton also participated in an exhibition which focused on a small

but increasingly significant group of studio artists. The show pointed the way to a new stage in his career. Exhibiting in *North Carolina Glass '76* as juror and guest speaker, Littleton toured the mountains of the state when he traveled to Western Carolina University to open the show. Visiting the area for the first time since the fifties, he was drawn by the beauty of the region around Penland School of Crafts, where his longtime friend Norm Schulman had made his home. Littleton had been contemplating leaving university teaching in order to concentrate on his creative work, and when Bess found in the Blue Ridge Mountains a setting reminiscent of her native Hawaii, the two wasted no time in deciding to move south. They bought a house and land high in the mountains within twenty minutes of Penland, and Littleton immediately began construction of a substantial glass studio, which has grown with a succession of additions over the years. Taking a leave of absence from the university, Littleton left for North Carolina in December 1976. The following spring, he was awarded the status of Professor Emeritus by the University of Wisconsin.

Littleton's primary reason for leaving university teaching was his desire to devote his energies to creating a body of work in glass. Increasingly troubled by the fact that faculty positions were no longer available to the students graduating from his program, he also wanted "to demonstrate that contemporary society is indeed willing to support the artist and that it is possible for a glass artist to earn a good living from the sale of his work." Littleton's decision came at a time of great activity in the worldwide market for glass, when increasing numbers of prominent galleries were choosing to center on that medium alone.

Thirty-five years earlier, Carl Milles could not have envisioned a future in which his young studio assistant at Cranbrook would lead a burgeoning market for sculpture in glass. The support which Littleton has received from collectors, galleries, and museums has freed him to create larger pieces. "The things that the artist sells point the way to where he is going," Littleton has said, an acknowledgment of an economic reality and an indication of the high regard in which he holds the collectors of his work. As his sculpture develops in the direction not only of increased scale but also of increased complexity, he stays one step ahead of the collectors in much the same way that he was challenged to stay ahead of his students when the studio movement was in its infancy.

The beauty of the Blue Ridge Mountains aside, Littleton could hardly have chosen a more stimulating location than the Penland area of North Carolina in which to make glass. Since the summer of 1965, when glassblowing was introduced to Penland School by Bill Boysen (then a Littleton student) many glass artists who have come to study or teach have settled in the mountains nearby. In the six years since the Littletons have joined the close-knit community of glass artists centered around Penland, the Spruce Pine studio has become a second focus of activity for the group. Making available his increasing battery of cold working equipment, Littleton has opened his shop to these younger colleagues, whom he regards as equals: "Helping one another and pushing one another . . . it's this kind of community that drives the artist, that keeps him going, keeps him stimulated." On a grand scale, Paris in the twenties was such a community, nourishing two forerunners of contemporary studio glass: Jean Sala and the highly influential Jean Marinot, to whom Littleton has been compared.[2]

Since moving to Spruce Pine, Littleton has involved himself intensely in studio work. The furnace he built in 1979 was based on the electric glass melting induction furnace using fused tin oxide electrodes that he built in 1974 with the assistance of a grant from the Corning Glass Works. Littleton acknowledges his debt to industry in technical areas, valuing the advice given him by experts John Bruns and John Wozinski of Corning in the construction of the prototype furnace in Verona which he had moved to North Carolina. The much larger Spruce Pine furnace borrowed another idea from industry, the use of two chambers separated by a perforated wall. Through this common hot wall glass constantly flows from the melting area into the working chamber, providing a continuous supply of high quality crystal. In autumn 1982 Littleton built the third electric furnace in the series, with a large door to accommodate bigger pieces. The scale of the current sculptures and the complexity of techniques involved require him to use two assistants in the furnace work, a situation that has enriched the Penland community by bringing promising young artists to the area. Gary Beecham has chosen to settle nearby and continues to assist Littleton in his work. More recently, Ken Carder joined Littleton in his studio.

Working in his new studio, without a second tank or pot furnace for melting colored glass as in the past, Littleton chose to use Kugler bars manufactured in a wide range of concentrated colors. In 1977, with the assistance of Fritz Dreisbach, he employed the traditional overlay technique for the first time, applying a thin layer of colored glass to the surface of a few sculptures in his loop series. Among the 1977 overlay pieces was *Inverted Tube/Cut Line,* shown in the Corning Museum's *New Glass: A Worldwide Survey.* A follow-up to the museum's *Glass '59,* this landmark exhibition demonstrated how far the studio glass movement had developed within its first two decades. In dramatic contrast to the previous exhibition—in which less than ten per cent of the work shown was submitted by studio glassworkers—*New Glass* included nine studio pieces to every one made by industry. A further indication of the vigor of the movement Littleton founded is that while fewer than two hundred glassmakers submitted entries to the exhibition in 1959, twenty years later the entrants totaled one thousand.

Littleton returned to the overlay technique in 1978, seeking to explore color relationships in his sculptures as he was doing in his prints. First applying a colored overlay to a crystal core, he then cased the piece in crystal; separating a sequence of overlays by gathers of his remarkably clear crystal in this manner, he achieved the effect of color suspended in light. So far, two series have developed from these explorations, both of which playfully reinterpret the artist's early study of mathematics. The solid geometry of the first series was gradually modulated by the fluidity of the medium itself to become the more bent and twisted topological forms which comprise the second series.

It has become clear that Littleton has attained the major goals of his career. This exhibition of his work, organized by the High Museum of Art and circulated to five other museums, is the culmination of a series of smaller retrospective exhibitions over the last five years. Major recognition of his sustained accomplishments as an artist came in 1978-79 when Littleton was awarded the Craftsman's Fellowship of the National Endowment for the Arts. Trustee Emeritus of the American Craft Council, Littleton recently received the highest honor bestowed by this organization, the Gold Medal—awarded only three times in the Council's history. Although he is no longer part of the educational system, hot glass programs are fully accepted in the curriculum of the university and his former students head many of this country's most influential departments.

And he has had the additional satisfaction of seeing his son John, together with Katherine Vogel, win international repute for their collaborative work in glass.

But if Littleton's life's work is well-rounded at this stage in his career, it is by no means complete. Greatly alive in his work, he has remarked "I am happy, because I see much to do ahead!" Continuing his contacts with artists overseas, Littleton travels widely and usually spends several weeks each year visiting Erwin Eisch in Frauenau. In the summer of 1981 he opened up his shop to visiting artists—including Eisch and Thomas Buechner, director of the Corning Museum of Glass—to experiment with printing from glass plates. So exciting were the results that in 1983 Littleton supervised the construction of a separate building to house the presses and growing print collection. Both students and artists of international renown visit the new studio to try their hands at the print medium.

Littleton's successes have multiplied the resources at his disposal. When Sybren Valkema spent a month blowing glass in Littleton's studio in the summer of 1983, he said "Everything is possible here, nothing is impossible. Don't try it—do it!" Today, the same conviction which set the studio glass movement in motion finds monumental expression in the art of Harvey Littleton.

Notes

[1]Joan Falconer Byrd, "Harvey Littleton, Pioneer in American Studio Glass," *American Craft*, Vol. 40, No. 1 (February/March, 1980), p. 2.

[2]Penelope Hunter-Stiebel, "Contemporary Art Glass: An Old Medium Gets a New Look," *Art News*, Vol. 80, No. 6 (Summer, 1981) p. 131.

Chronology

1922: Born in Corning, New York

1936: Began Elmira College extension classes in art

1939-40: Studied physics at University of Michigan

1941: Studied at Cranbrook Academy of Art (spring semester)

1941-42: Studied industrial design at University of Michigan

1942-45: Served with U.S. Army Signal Corps in Africa, Italy, and France; received commendation from Chief Signal Officer in Europe

1945: Studied at Brighton School of Art, England, for three months with Norah Bradon and others

1946: Torso modeled at Brighton School of Art cast in Multiform glass by the artist at Corning Glass Works

1946-47: Studied industrial design at University of Michigan

1947: Received BD degree from University of Michigan; submitted proposal to Corning Glass Works (funding denied); married Bess Tamura

1947-49: Partner, Corporate Designers, Inc., Ann Arbor, Michigan; taught in private pottery which became Ann Arbor Potters' Guild

1949-51: Taught ceramics at the Museum School, Toledo Museum of Art, Toledo, Ohio; founded Toledo Potters' Guild; studied ceramics at Cranbrook Academy of Art with Maija Grotell; received MFA degree

1951: Bought eighty-acre farm in Verona, Wisconsin; converted farm building to studio

1951-77: Faculty member, Department of Art and Art Education, University of Wisconsin, Madison

1953: Exhibited ceramics in *Designer Craftsmen U.S.A.,* sponsored by American Craft Council

1954: Founded Midwest Designer-Craftsmen with Michael and Frances Higgins and others; received University of Wisconsin research committee grant for study of vapor glazing; exhibited in *Ceramic National,* Syracuse Museum of Art, receiving American Art Clay purchase award

1956: Exhibited in *First International Exposition of Ceramics,* Cannes, France

1957: Visited Jugtown Pottery, Seagrove, North Carolina

1957-58: Trustee, American Craft Council; received University of Wisconsin research committee travel grant for study of Islamic influence on contemporary Spanish pottery; met Jean Sala in Paris; visited glass factories in Naples and Murano, Italy

1958: Melted first glass in ceramics kiln in studio in Verona, Wisconsin

1959: Chairman of glass panel at Third National Conference of the American Craft Council; established Paoli Clay Company

1959-64: Trustee, American Craft Council

1960-61: Half-time leave from University of Wisconsin; built glass studio on farm in Verona

1961: Presented paper at Fourth National Conference of the American Craft Council, "A Potter's Experience with Glass"

1962: Conducted two seminar-workshops in glassblowing at Toledo Museum of Art; made survey of European schools teaching hot glass, funded by grants from University of Wisconsin research committee and Toledo Museum of Art; visited Jean Sala in Paris; met Erwin Eisch in Frauenau, Bavaria

1962-63: Taught first two classes of University of Wisconsin students in glass studio in Verona; lectured widely on hot glass in Midwest and Northeast

1963: One-man exhibition of glass at Art Institute of Chicago; secured funding, rented and equipped space for student studio in Madison

1964: Exhibition at Museum of Contemporary Crafts, New York City; demonstrated glassblowing at first meeting of World Congress of Craftsmen, Columbia University, New York City; exhibition at Corning Museum of Glass, Corning, New York; exhibited in *13th Triennale,* Milan, Italy

1964-67: Chairman, Department of Art and Art Education, University of Wisconsin

1967-68: Year's leave of absence from University of Wisconsin, funded by research committee grant; Eisch worked one month in Littleton's studio

1968: Turned to minimalism in reaction to influence of Eisch; presented paper at Eighth International Glass Congress, London; visited Eisch in Frauenau; made thirty pieces for exhibition in Europe

1969: Exhibition with Eisch at Handwerkskammer in Munich and Cologne; exhibition at Lee Nordness Galleries, New York City, beginning four-year association

1969-71: Chairman, Department of Art and Art Education, University of Wisconsin

1970-71: Awarded Louis Comfort Tiffany Foundation Grant with Michael Taylor, apprentice

1971: Publication of *Glassblowing: A Search for Form,* Van Nostrand-Reinhold, New York; attended Ninth International Glass Congress, Versailles; saw Jean Sala for last time at Epône, France

1972: Received University of Wisconsin research committee grant; worked at Val Saint-Lambert, Belgium; exhibited pieces made at the Val with work of Georges Collignon at Maison de Culture, Liège, Belgium; awarded Honorary Membership, National Council for Education in the Ceramic Arts, U.S.A.

1973: Guest artist, Gerrit Rietveld Academy, Amsterdam, Holland; conducted seminar, Royal College of Art, London; exhibited in *15th Triennale,* Milan, Italy

1974: Worked at Eisch studio for six weeks; exhibition with Eisch at J. & L. Lobmeyr,

Vienna, Austria; directed summer workshop-seminar on cold working, funded by grants from National Endowment for the Arts, Steuben Glass Works, and Corning Glass Works Foundation; began printing from glass plates with assistance of James Pernotto; received grant from Corning Glass Works for construction of electric glass melting induction furnace for the studio artist

1975: Received University of Wisconsin research committee grant to develop printing from glass plates; elected Fellow of Collegium of Craftsmen of American Craft Council; visiting professor, University of California, Los Angeles

1975-76: Retrospective Exhibition, Bergstrom Art Center, Neenah, Wisconsin, which later traveled to Charles H. MacNider Museum, Mason City, Iowa

1976: Received Honorary Life Membership, Glass Art Society, U.S.A.; moved to Spruce Pine, North Carolina

1977: Took leave of absence from University of Wisconsin spring semester; granted Professor Emeritus status; exhibited at Contemporary Art Glass Gallery, New York City, first of recurring exhibitions

1978: Exhibited at Habatat Galleries, Dearborn, Michigan, first of recurring exhibitions

1978-79: Awarded National Endowment for the Arts Craftsman's Fellowship

1979: Traveling exhibition organized by Mint Museum of Art, Charlotte

1982: Awarded Honorary Doctorate of Fine Arts, Philadelphia College of Art; retrospective exhibition, Heller Gallery, New York City; retrospective exhibition, The Works Gallery, Philadelphia

1983: Awarded Gold Medal of American Craft Council; retrospective exhibition at Institute for Contemporary Art, Florida State University, Tallahassee; elected to Board of Trustees of Penland School of Crafts, Penland, North Carolina

The Works

Harvey Littleton's career as an artist now spans more than thirty years: his oeuvre is vast. He was nationally known for his ceramics when he began to work in glass. However, the pottery stands as prologue to the major thrust of his career and shows little of the vitality of his glass sculpture. The first five years after he introduced hot glass as a studio medium was a period of extensive experimentation for Littleton, a time for developing skills and establishing his personal vocabulary of form. Thereafter, though he continued to take chances and change direction, we are always dealing with the work of a mature master.

An analysis of Littleton's work into discrete categories is problematical. His career is marked by periods when he produced very disciplined, rational pieces, followed by outbursts of passion. He sometimes pursued several lines of development at the same time. A coherent chronology of form is further complicated by his commitment to continual "artistic exploration" and by the fact that furnace-worked components frequently "lie around the studio for months unfinished," until he understands them well enough to use them in a sculpture.

The illustrations which follow are grouped with an eye to the forms and techniques which have recurred at intervals in Littleton's career. Thus, though the catalogue numbers assigned in the exhibition list (page 102) reflect the order in which the works were produced, the arrangement of the illustrations and the commentaries which accompany them have more to do with techniques and with formal relationships among the works than with strict chronology.

Cast Torsos

Littleton's figurative sculpture melds two important early influences: his academic background in sculpture and his employment as a moldmaker in the Vycor Multiform Glass Laboratory at the Corning Glass Works. The multiform material, a 96% silica glass, was similar to *pâte de verre*. A mold was made and the sculpture was slip cast; after drying, the piece was fused in a furnace. Although the artist dismisses the earlier torso (no. 1) as a student work, the sculpture cast in January 1946 (no. 2) was the first Littleton piece to be exhibited. Four castings were made of this sculpture under the artist's control, and of these the most finished is the first, shown here.

Littleton's excitement at the translation of the torso into the translucent material remains vivid: "After the piece was fired I rubbed some of the surface with carborundum, and then I took an oxygen torch and fused the surface. Then I dulled it again with hydrofluoric acid to take the bright shine off. There was a certain refinement of the surface, and it had a lot more light transmission than the opaque clay."

1

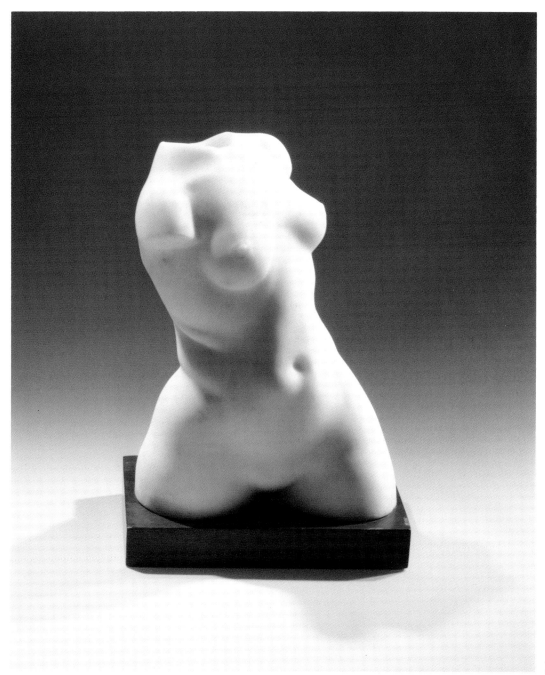

2

Stoneware and Porcelain

Throughout thirteen years as a ceramic artist, Littleton made functional ware almost exclusively. He had built two wood kilns by the time he received his MFA degree from Cranbrook Academy in 1951, and he consistently favored a simple and direct approach to throwing, glazing, and firing his work. His palette was composed of earth tones, and he used slips and oxides of iron, manganese, and cobalt. He decorated his pieces as they turned on the potter's wheel, emphasizing the contour of the thrown form. His exploration of salt glazing grew out of his involvement with wood kilns. The salt glazing process, little used in the fifties, is based upon the volatilization of salt thrown into the hot kiln and its reaction with the clay to form a glaze. The directness of Littleton's techniques point to the artistic economy of his work in glass.

3

4

5

6

7

9

10

11

Cut Pieces and Functional Forms

The techniques of grinding and polishing were familiar to Littleton more than ten years before he first blew glass, and a continuing interest in the cold working processes has marked his development. When Littleton first melted glass in his studio in Verona, he ground and polished the resulting pieces of cullet to demonstrate the sculptural potential of glass (no. 8). While the cullet made in these first melts was yellowish and of low quality, the crystal with which he worked at Val Saint-Lambert in 1972 (see no. 41) had a startling purity which was displayed most effectively when the glass was faceted and polished.

Although "never really interested in the function of glass," Littleton concentrated on making traditional, symmetrical forms while he was teaching himself glassblowing. Repeating basic exercises in control, Littleton took advantage of the reliability and long-working properties of the #475 glass marbles developed by Labino. The addition of the same colorants he had used in ceramics—copper for blue green, manganese for purple, cobalt for blue—heightened the appeal of the pieces.

At this stage, even the simplest form represented an important achievement. The oil drop paperweight (no. 14) recapitulates the initial steps in glassblowing. The artist makes the first gather of molten glass from the furnace on the hollow blowpipe which he rotates in his hand. After rolling the glass on the metal plate (or marver) to chill it, he sends a small puff of air down the pipe and heat expands the breath into a round and neatly-centered bubble within the glass. After a second gather is added, the blob of glass (or parison) is rolled within a wet fruitwood block carved in the shape of a bowl. The bubble must remain on center; watching the fading glow of the cooling glass, the artist must judge the right moment to expand the bubble of air within the stiffening form. After the piece is softened by reheating, the glass blower uses a tweezer-like tool called a jack to pinch the form where it attaches to the blowpipe, and the bubble is sealed off. The narrow neck, chilled by metal tools, is broken by a sharp rap on the pipe, and the piece is transferred to an electric annealing oven for slow cooling. The drop of oil introduced in the forming process defines the blown bubble by carbonizing its surface. All the processes of glassblowing demand sensitivity and a highly developed sense of timing.

8

13

14

15

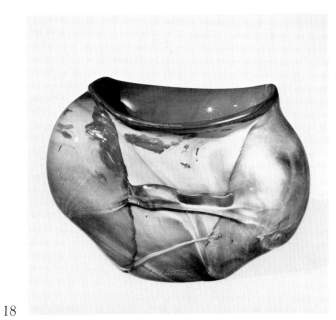

18

44

58

41

The Atlanta showing of *Harvey K. Littleton: A Retrospective Exhibition*, and the educational programs and events, and catalogue accompanying have been made possible through the generosity of

Park

35

expression in the medium, Littleton "physically attacked the glass. But I liked it: I'd been conditioned to like broken edges." In these pieces Littleton violated everything that painstaking discipline had taught him about glassblowing technique. Rather than working for the even distribution of heat throughout the form, he would subject an area of the piece to the direct flame of the gas burner. Drawing on the blowpipe, he could collapse the wall inward; a sharp breath outward would explode the form. He exploited uneven thicknesses of glass, which responded differently to temperature change and to the centrifugal force generated by a rapidly rotated blowpipe. These works exploit chance. At the same time, they demonstrate Littleton's contention: "You don't enshrine the accident, you build on it."

16

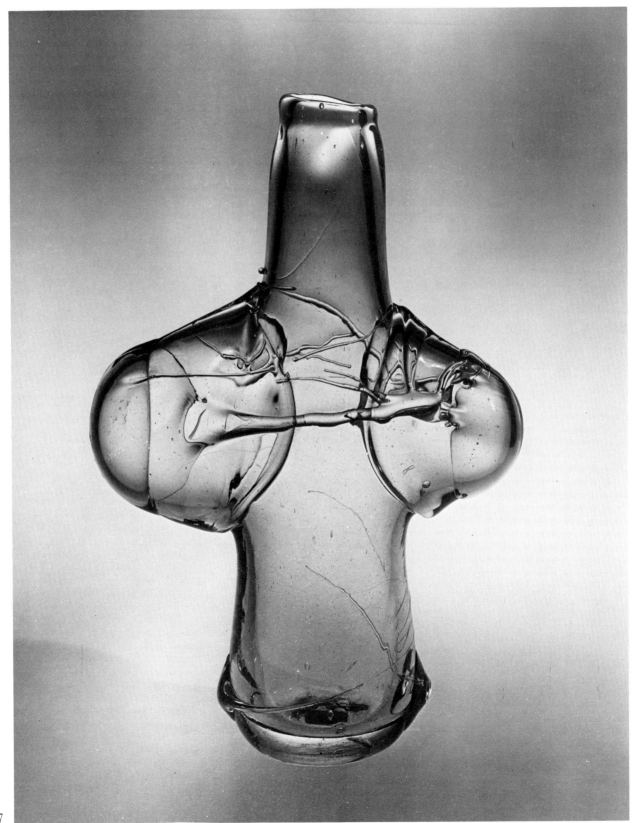

17

24

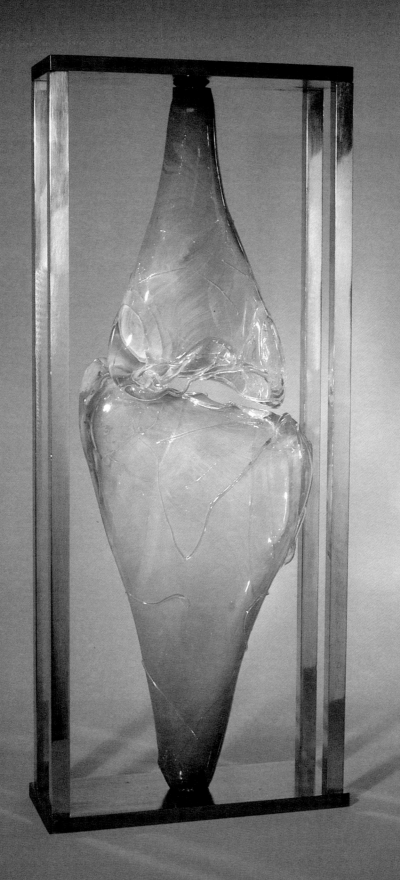

Tubes, Rods, Columns, and Eyes

In direct reaction to the formal complexity of his earlier work, strongly influenced by Eisch, Littleton turned to minimal statements in early 1968. Blown forms were elongated by the action of gravity and by the pull of centrifugal forces generated by swinging the blowpipe. Sliced off at top and bottom, the blown forms became tubes. Cold working techniques became more important to the artist, who began to assemble tubes and drawn rods on bases of black plate glass or machined metal.

As Littleton focused on a new vocabulary of form, he began to melt his own glass, searching for the particular working properties and the brilliance he required. His tubes became more slender and less severe (see no. 29). The pieces grew larger and the hollow tube evolved into the column (see no. 32).

The earliest of Littleton's eye forms (no. 39) dates from the period of the tubes and rods, and the series shares the geometric precision of these pieces. The forms grew directly out of the artist's interest in the optic properties of glass: "The cut surface lets you see into the wall of the hemisphere, and the light is concentrated by the curving sides and reflected back out the cut edge. This gives a rich, deep, intense colored circle of light." (*Glassblowing: A Search for Form*, p. 47.)

27

28

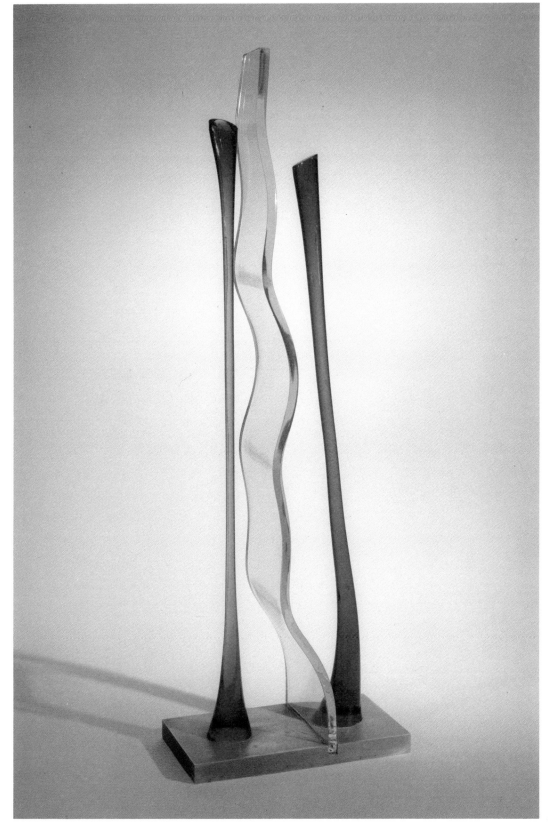

35

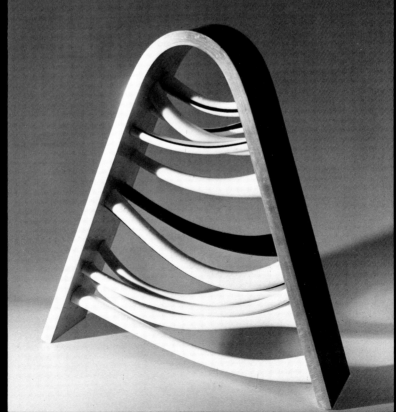

38

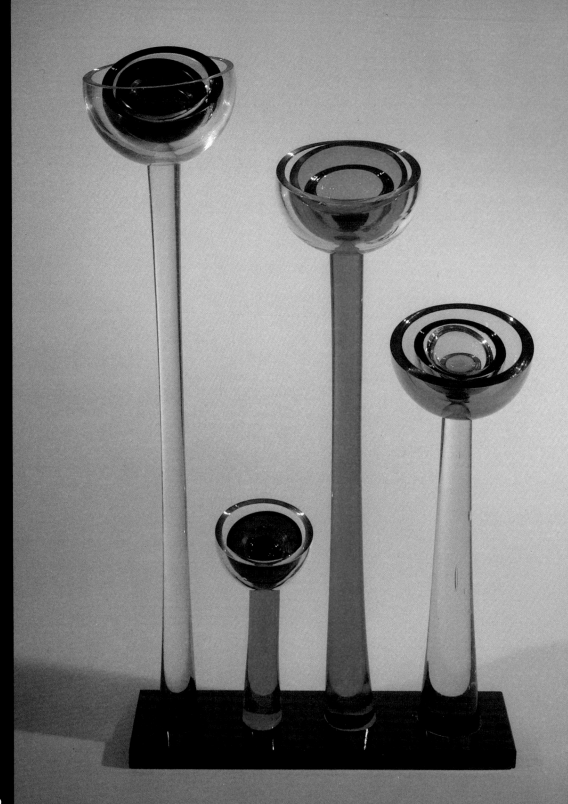

Folded Forms and Loops

Littleton's folded forms were produced by bending tubes upon themselves while they were hot on the blowpipe. The pieces made in opal glass relied on cutting to reveal their soft convolutions: the slicing of the form made an effective counterpoint to the spontaneity of the furnace work. In *Amber Crested Form* (no. 51), an irregular prunt was added to the folded form.

The loops formed an important series in Littleton's creative production for more than ten years. Although the first sculptures in the series were made in the mid-sixties, the real impetus for the development came from Littleton's work with tubes and cylinders in 1969. The elongation of these forms was accomplished by holding the pipe straight down, so that gravity would extend the hot glass directly in line with the blowpipe or punty. If the softened form was balanced upright on the pipe, the elongated tube would fall into a graceful arc, carving out a harmonious negative space as it descended. Inverted on a high base the curve became a U-form (no. 52); mounted on its side, a "C" (no. 45). Making many forms in the same color, Littleton would select, cut, and compose them on a plate glass base (see no. 36). The loops became more dynamic as the columns became more attenuated. The fall of the molten glass on the pipe was arrested at floor level by a graphite slab at the artist's feet, terminating the column in a voluptuous fullness of form. His *Loop Form* (no. 57) is a virtuoso statement of tension. *Triple Loops* (no. 62), one of the final sculptures of the series, represents one of the artist's first uses of the overlay technique, and the loops are free of attachment to a base.

26

31

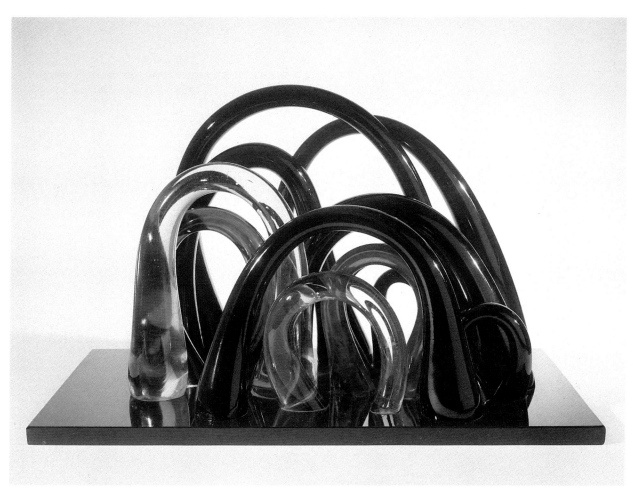

36

37

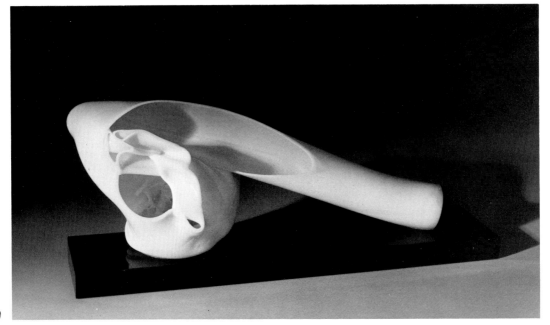

40

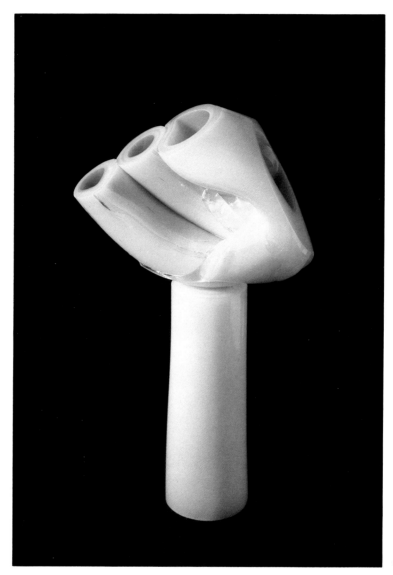

46

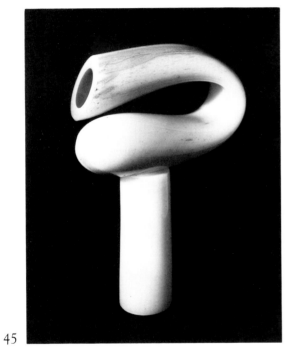

45

52

50

51

54

57

56

Plate Glass, Optic Glass, and Lens Discs

Littleton began bending or slumping plate glass in an annealing oven to produce bases for his sculptures. Then he began to integrate the pieces more fully with the furnace-worked components (see *Pile Up,* no. 61). Slumping did not require the use of the furnace (which was expensive to operate), and large pieces assembled out of plate glass could be safely taken apart, transported, and reassembled at an exhibition site. In *Distortion Box II* (no. 47) and *Do Not Spindle* (no. 49), bent glass squares are separated by brass spacers with a nylon washer on either side and with a brass rod running through the middle. The clear glass is defined by its edges, while its refractive properties distort the cylindrical brass form.

Littleton began another group of slumped pieces by bending massive bars of optic glass (made for use in a telescope): the important mobile piece *Rock Around the Clock* (no. 60) belongs to this group. The friction of glass on glass is so slight that, set in motion, the piece rocks for a full hour. Littleton's plans for an extended series of large sculptures based on slumping were crowded out by his enthusiasm for working hot glass: "As soon as the furnace is on, you forget that kind of thing." His latest use of preformed industrial glass involved lens discs given to him by one of the plants of the Corning Glass Works. After several years of seeing the lens blanks in the studio, he cut and sandblasted them, using them with furnace-worked forms (nos. 86, 88, 89).

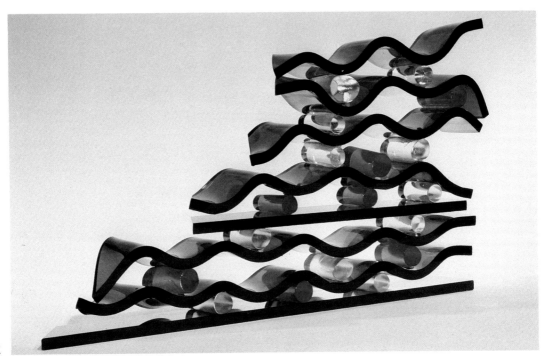

42

43

48

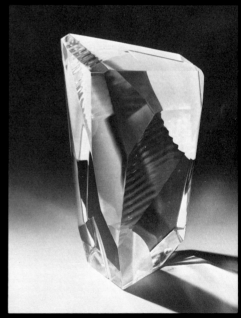

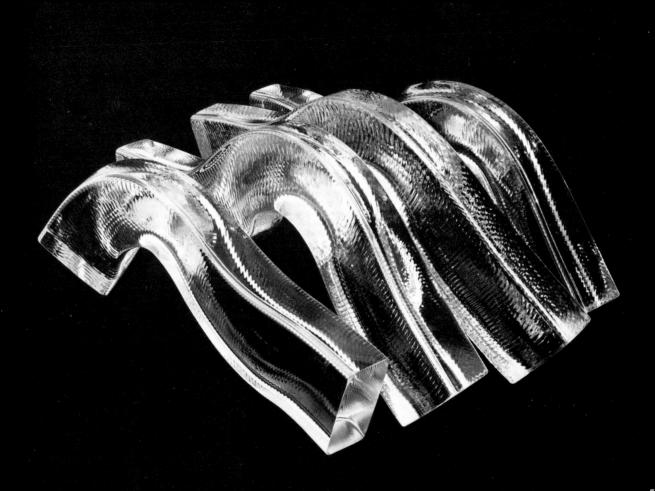

60

61

Solid Geometry

The solid geometry series began in 1978, when Littleton returned to the overlay technique in order to explore color relationships in his sculpture. The overlay is applied to a cylinder of crystal on the punty by first adhering to the flattened end of the cylinder a colored shape resembling an open bowl. After reheating, the Kugler colored form is inverted with a wooden paddle and drawn over the cylinder to sheath it in intense color. The overlay is fused to the clear core, and a gather of glass from the furnace cases the color in crystal. An early piece in the series, *Positive-Negative* (no. 63), contrasts two slices of the cased form: the flattened end of the original cylinder with its overlay displays a vivid magenta circle; next to it stands a cross section of the cylinder, its wall defined by the thin ring of the colored overlay.

In later pieces Littleton applied a sequence of overlays, casing each color in crystal. Sliced across, the overlays appear as concentric circles of color suspended in light. The optic properties of the heavy, highly polished glass multiply the views of the forms within. The sculptures are no longer attached to a base. Littleton says he "got to worrying about glue." More importantly, he has come to feel that the relationship between the forms need not be predetermined and should allow for decision and discovery on the part of the viewer—that the collector of a sculpture should have a part in creating the piece (see no. 97).

64

63

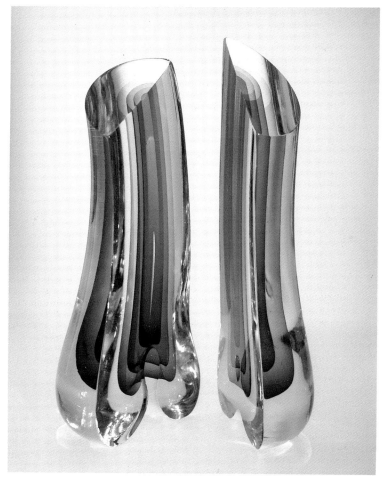

66

67

73

68

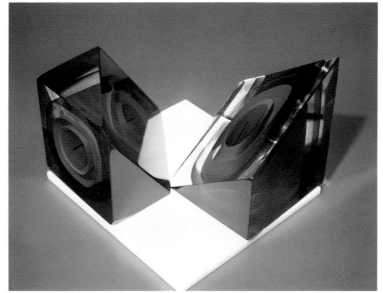

69

75

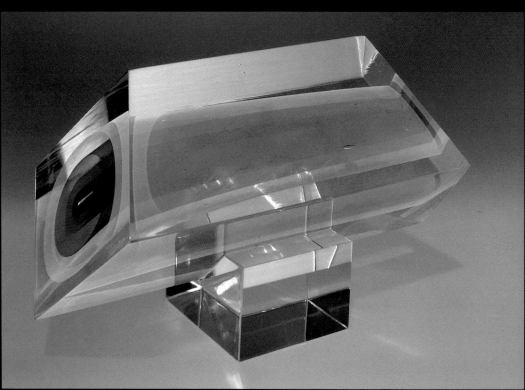

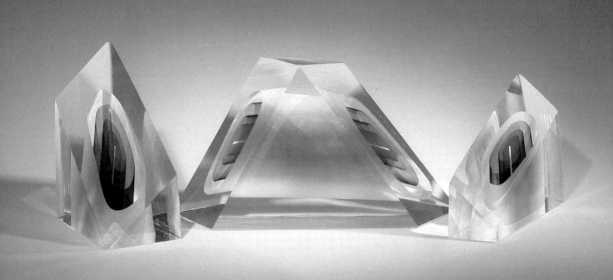

Topological Geometry

Littleton's most recent works show a complexity and energy similar to his loops. *Ruby Twisted Column* (no. 74) was one of the first of this new series, in which the precision of the concentric overlays is played against the dynamism of the form. "The bending in my pieces," Littleton has said, "especially if it doesn't follow a rigid formula, begins to be topological geometry." The concept is beautifully expressed by the movement and flow of glass. In 1983, Littleton wrote: "Flattening the basic ovoid, extending and rotating the soft form against the drag of its inertia—these are elements that give birth to a range of forms I am now exploiting." In the crowns (nos. 87, 98), the multiple forms achieve the monumentality to which Littleton has aspired throughout his career as a sculptor.

75

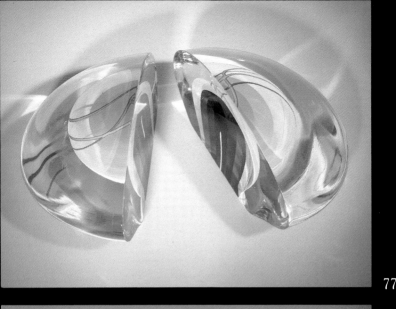

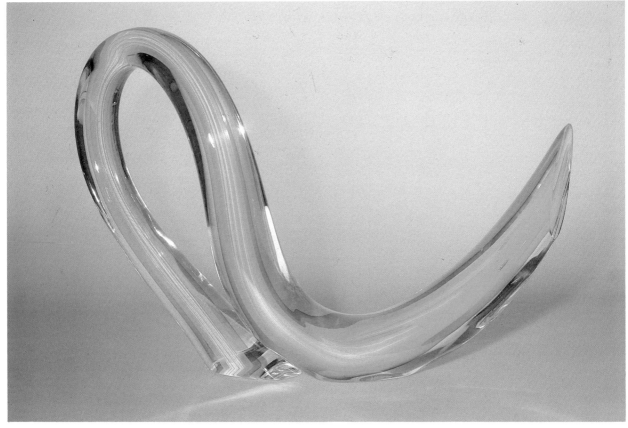

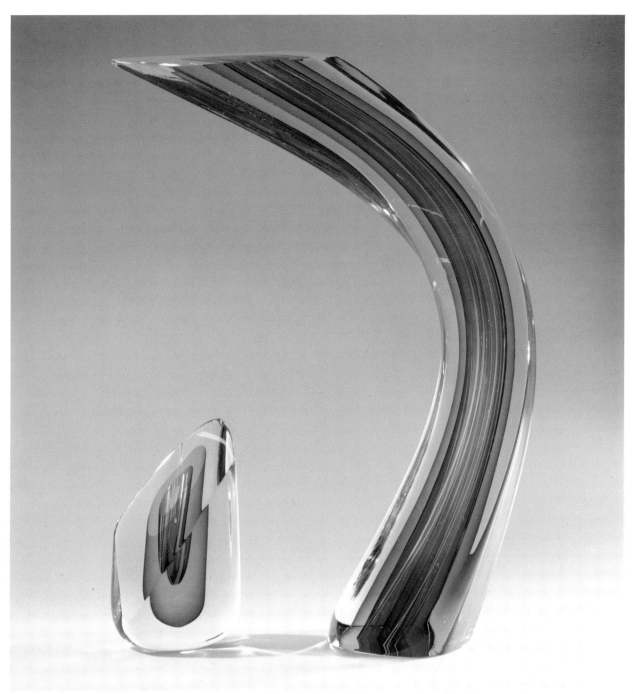

82

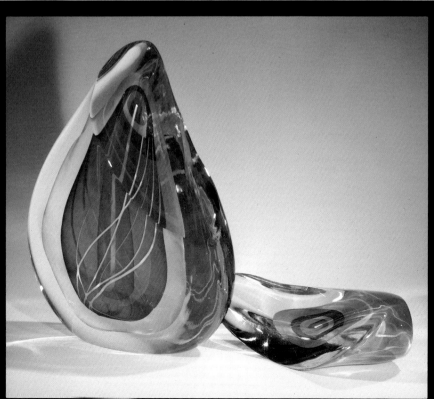

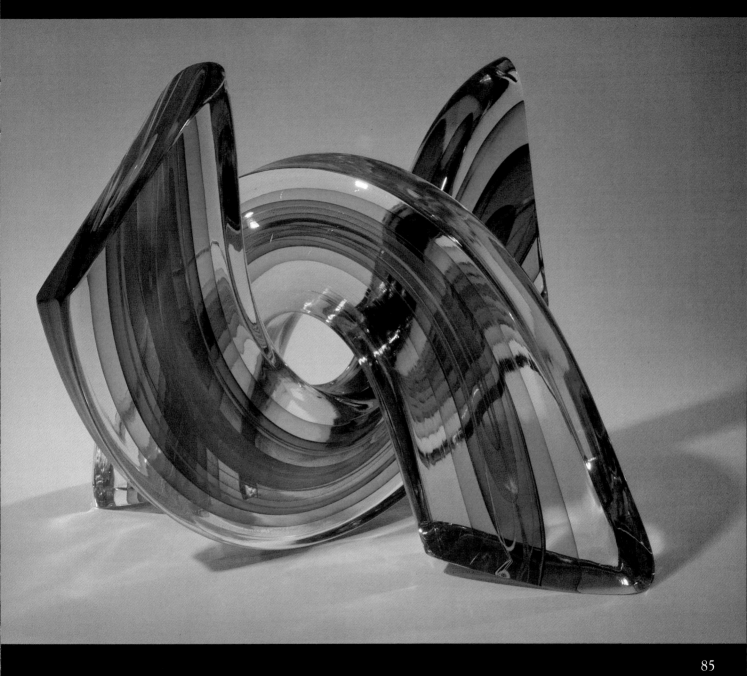

87

88

91

96

91

89

94

95

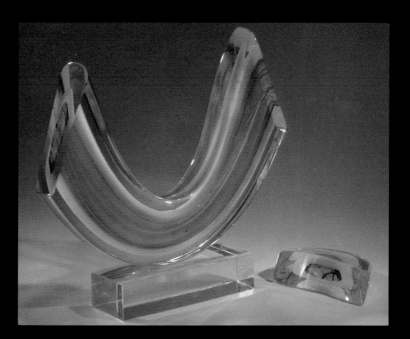

97

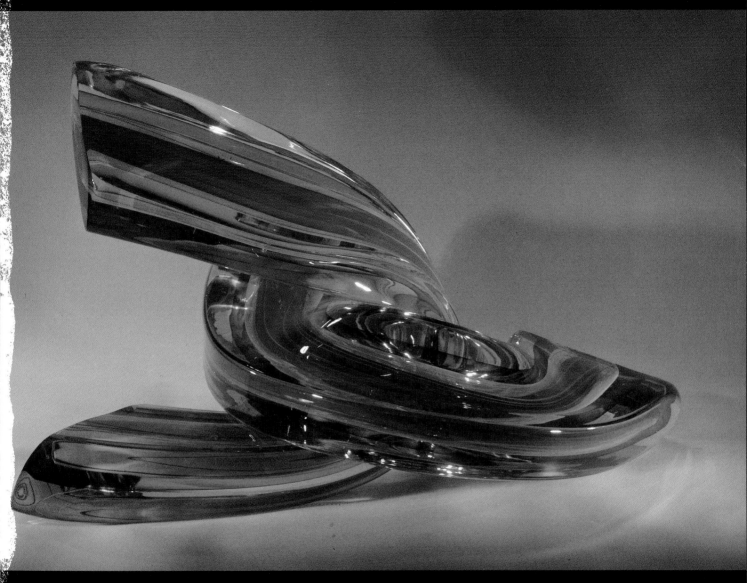

100

101

Intaglio Prints

Printing from glass plates was suggested to Littleton by his sandblasting experiments in 1974. Among the advantages of glass are the perfect elasticity of the material, which allows the plate to return to its original form after printing, and the fact that glass does not react with colored inks, as frequently happens with metal. Color printing from glass excited Littleton, and a new interest in color infused his sculpture beginning with *Glass Spectrum* (no. 43).

Littleton's prints do not begin with drawing. He points out that "their origin is in glass and in the manipulation of color. My best prints are built as a sculptor builds sculpture." The prints fall into three categories. The early experiments, represented by *Trial I* and *Trial II* (nos. 102, 103), suggest Abstract Expressionism. As in his sculptures, Littleton reacted to this early complexity with simplification, limiting himself to minimal forms. The *10° Rotation Suite* (no. 105) and *Origami Suite* (no. 108) use geometric shapes as the format for color studies. There is a strong formal relationship between these prints and earlier plate glass sculptures such as *Triangulation* (no. 48), in which Littleton's imagination appears at its most rational. *00 Buckshot* and *#6 Birdshot* (nos. 106, 107) represent the third category of prints, those which deal with the theme of breakage. In making these plates, Littleton fractured safety glass with a shotgun blast, then worked with the breakage lines.

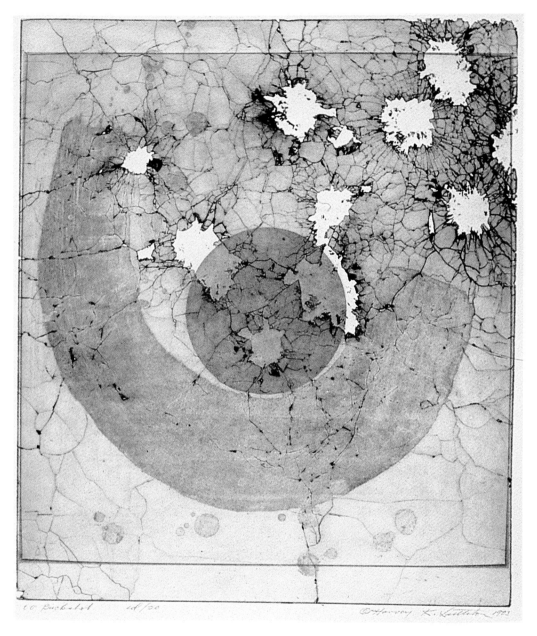

C O Buchertal   ed/30   ©Harvey K. Littleton 1983   106

Catalogue of the Exhibition

Works are listed in chronological order. Dimensions are given in inches, height before width before depth. Works are in the collection of the artist unless otherwise noted.

1. *Torso*, 1942
Opaque white glass, slipcast of Vycor Multiform glass at Corning Glass Works, 11¼ x 5 x 5, The Corning Museum of Glass, gift of Dr. and Mrs. Fred A. Bickford

2. *Torso*, 1946
Modeled at Brighton School of Art, England, opaque white glass, slipcast of Vycor Multiform glass at Corning Glass Works, 11 x 8 x 5½, Arnot Art Museum, Elmira, New York

3. *Vase*, 1950
Stoneware with iron red glaze, 12 x 11 x 11, The University of Michigan Museum of Art, gift of the artist

4. *Stoneware Vase*, 1954
Red and black glaze, 14 x 9 x 9, Everson Museum of Art, Syracuse, New York, purchase, 1962

5. *Untitled*, 1956
Stoneware bowl with iron wax resist decoration, 3½ x 10½ x 10½

6. *Salt Glaze Bottle*, 1957
Stoneware clay made and bisque fired in Wisconsin, salt glaze fired at Jugtown, N.C., decorated with Albany slip and manganese carbonate lines, 7 x 6 x 6

7. *Stoneware Bowl*, ca. 1960
Dolomitic limestone glaze, wax resist stained with iron sulfate, 9½ x 14 x 14

8. *Glass Pieces*, 1960
Carved from lumps of cullet of lead glass, later addition of base, 5¾ x 4½ x 4½

9. *Stoneware Vase*, 1960
Dolomitic glaze, wax resist decorated with iron sulfate, 13½ x 6½ x 6½

10. *Stoneware Teapot*, 1961
Temmoku glaze, 5 x 8 x 8

11. *Porcelain Bowl*, 1961
Dolomitic glaze, wax resist decoration stained with iron sulfate, 5 x 8 x 8

12. *Stoneware Vase*, 1961
Ash glaze, underglaze decoration of Albany slip with 10% cobalt carbonate, 10 x 6 x 5, The Arthur E. Baggs Memorial Library, Ohio State University

13. *Bud Vase*, 1962
Glass from #475 marbles colored with copper blue with manganese stripes, 7½ x 2½ x 2¼

14. *Paperweight*, 1963
Glass from #475 marbles with oil drop, 3½ x 3 x 3

15. *Vase*, 1963
Glass from #475 marbles, rolled in cobalt carbonate between gathers, 5¾ x 2½ x 1

16. *Implosion/Explosion*, 1964
Glass from #475 marbles colored with copper oxides and reduced, 7½ x 5½ x 5½

17. *Cross Vase*, 1964
Blue/green clear glass from #475 marbles, 12 x 8½ x 3½

18. *Vase*, 1965
Glass from #475 marbles colored with silver oxide, 4½ x 7 x 4, The Corning Museum of Glass

19. *Yellow Anthropomorphic Vase*, 1965
Glass from #475 marbles, prunts colored with silver oxide, 11 x 7½ x 4, Helen P. Hooper

20. *Y Form Sculpture*, 1965
Glass from #475 marbles colored with cobalt oxide on marble base, 13½ x 8½ x 2½

21. *Vase with Expanded Prunts*, 1965
Glass from #475 marbles colored with silver oxides, 6¼ x 7½ x 4½

22. *Copper Grey Form*, 1965
Glass from #475 marbles colored with copper sulfate on white marble base, 13 x 9 x 7, Mr. and Mrs. S. K. Heninger, Jr.

23. *Exploded Form*, 1965
Glass from #475 marbles colored with silver oxides on aluminum base, 18 x 7 x 5, Mr. and Mrs. S. K. Heninger, Jr.

24. *Imploded Form*, 1966
Glass from #475 marbles with cobalt on travertine base, 18 x 6 x 6

25. *Symphony in Yellow*, 1966
Glass from #475 marbles colored with silver oxides, expanded prunts, steel and brass frame, 24½ x 10 x 3½, Maurine B. Littleton

26. *Copper Schmeltz Glass Form*, 1966
Glass from #475 marbles colored with copper oxide, 7 7/16 x 4 1/16 x 1 9/16, National Museum of American History, Smithsonian Institution (shown in Washington only)

27. *Cut Cylinders*, 1968
Cut clear cylinders of barium/potash glass on stainless steel and bronze plate glass base, 9¾ x 5½ x 5¾

28. *Classic Symbol*, 1968
Barium/potash glass drawn and cut rods with copper ring on aluminum base, 28 x 10½ x 11, Mr. and Mrs. Samuel C. Johnson

29. *Falling Blue*, 1969
Cut barium/potash glass tubes colored with copper oxide assembled on bronze plate glass base, 21 x 13 x 8, Collection of the American Craft Museum, gift of the Johnson Wax Co., from *Objects: USA*

30. *Reflections*, 1969
Barium/potash glass drawn and cut rods on forged steel stand, 60 x 34 x 25, The Prairie School, Racine, Wisconsin

31. *Mobile Form*, 1969
Glass from #475 marbles on bronze plate glass base, 7 x 6½ x 3

32. *Column III*, 1970
Selenium glass on aluminum base, 52 x 5 x 5, The Toledo Museum of Art, Toledo, Ohio

33. *Sympathetic Movement*, 1970
Bent plate glass with copper blue rods of barium/potash glass on aluminum base, 33 x 11½ x 6

34. *Fallen Purple*, 1970
Manganese tubes and rods of barium/potash glass on bent plate glass, 11 x 20 x 12½

35. *Triumph*, 1970
Copper blue barium/potash glass and aluminum, 15½ x 17½ x 4, The Bergstrom-Mahler Museum, Neenah, Wisconsin, gift of Friends of Bergstrom, 1976

36. *Opportunity Trap*, 1970
Drawn glass rods on bronze plate glass, 13 x 22⅜ x 12 1/16, Huntington Galleries, Huntington, West Virginia

37. *Black on White*, 1971
Black and white opal glass cullet from Fostoria on bronze plate glass base, 12⅞ x 21 x 9¾, Mack L. Graham

38. *Black and White Web*, 1971
White and black opal glass cullet from Fostoria with aluminum, 20 x 18 x 4

39. *Mary Mary*, 1971
Blown and cut barium/potash glass with various coloring oxides on bronze plate glass base, 23⅛ x 13¼ x 5, Memphis Brooks Museum of Art, Eugenia Buxton Whitnel Funds

40. *White Folded Form*, 1972
Opal white Fostoria cullet, cut and polished on bronze plate glass base, 5 x 12½ x 3½

41. *Glass Sculpture 1972*, 1972
Made at Val Saint-Lambert, Seraing, Belgium, cut and polished lead crystal, 18½ x 4 x 4, Carola Eisenbeis Van Ham, Kassel, West Germany

42. *Pile Up*, 1972-73
Copper blue and crystal barium/potash rods with ground, polished and bent bronze plate glass, 19 x 38 x 6, S. C. Johnson and Son, Inc., Racine, Wisconsin

43. *Glass Spectrum*, 1974
Stained glass with aluminum, 32 x 26 x 6

44. *Selenium Amber Cut Vase*, 1974
Selenium glass, made at demonstration of the cold working seminar, sponsored by University of Wisconsin-Madison and Corning Glass Foundation at Littleton's studio, Verona, Wisconsin, 4½ x 5 x 5

45. *Opal "C" Form*, 1974
Opal glass with silver nitrate decoration, made at the Eisch Factory in Frauenau, West Germany, 7 x 7 x 3

46. *Opaque White Form*, 1974
Opal glass with silver nitrate decoration, made at the Eisch Factory, Frauenau, West Germany, 14½ x 8½ x 4

47. *Distortion Box II*, 1974
Bent plate glass with brass fittings, 15 x 15 x 24, Elvehjem Museum of Art, University of Wisconsin-Madison

48. *Triangulation*, 1974
Bronze plate glass with brass fittings, 48 x 48 x 12

49. *Do Not Spindle*, 1975
Bent plate glass with brass fittings, 18 x 12 x 12, Dr. and Mrs. Sheldon M. Barnett

50. *Amber Twist*, 1976
Barium/potash glass with enamel white thread, 17½ high, The Metropolitan Museum of Art, gift of Joseph H. Hazen Foundation, Inc., 1978

51. *Amber Crested Form*, 1976
Barium/potash glass with selenium, 16½ high, The Metropolitan Museum of Art, gift of William D. and Rose D. Barker

52. *U Form*, 1977
Barium/potash glass with gold-ruby lines, 14½ x 6½ x 4

53. *Four Seasons*, 1977
Barium/potash glass with various coloring oxides, 5½ x 14 x 12, Paul and Elmerina Parkman

54. *Progression*, 1977
Barium/potash glass with dark blue and white Kugler color cores, 10 x 10 x 6½

55. *Optic Wave*, 1978
Bent optic glass bar manufactured by Corning Glass Works, Danville, Virginia, 10½ x 32 x 18

56. *Sympathy*, 1978
Barium/potash glass with cased double overlay of Kugler colors drawn and cut on a lead optic glass base, 16 x 10 x 8½, High Museum of Art, Atlanta, gift of the artist

57. *Loop Form*, 1978
Barium/potash glass with cased double overlay of Kugler color on plate glass base, 16½ x 14 x 4½

58. *Melon Cut Spheres*, 1978
Cut and textured barium/potash glass blown vase forms, 5 x 5½, 5 x 5, and 4½ x 4, Mr. and Mrs. Edward E. Elson

59. *Crested Schizoid Form*, 1978
Kugler color double underlay, cut barium/potash glass on white opal glass base, 13½ x 8 x 7, Gordon B. Mott and Merrily A. Smith

60. *Rock Around the Clock*, 1978
Bent optic glass bar manufactured by Corning Glass Works, Danville, Virginia, with a barium/potash glass cylinder on bronze plate glass base, two pieces, 8 x 24½ x 6½, Andrew D. Heineman

61. *Pile Up*, 1979
Bent optic glass bars manufactured by Corning Glass Works, Danville, Virginia, aluminum cylinder on bronze plate glass base, 10½ x 31½ x 22⅞, The Corning Museum of Glass, purchased with the aid of funds from the National Endowment for the Arts

62. *Triple Loops*, 1979
Barium/potash glass with cased Kugler color overlay, 14¾ x 14½ x 7, Mr. and Mrs. Richard Handelsman

63. *Postive-Negative,* 1979
Cased Kugler color overlay, barium/potash glass cut and polished with engraved line, 2½ x 2½ x 1

64. *Oblique Section,* 1979
Barium/potash glass with multiple cased overlays of Kugler colors: yellow, ruby, blue, white center line, 5½ x 4½ x 4¾

65. *Cut Optic Form,* 1980
Clear optic crystal, cut from bars manufactured by Corning Glass Works, Danville, Virginia, 7½ x 5 x 4

66. *Witch of Agnesi II,* 1980
Barium/potash glass with multiple cased overlays of Kugler colors: ruby, red, blue, opal white, white center line, 13 x 6 x 2½ and 12½ x 6 x 3

67. *90° Arc Segment,* 1980
Barium/potash glass with multiple case overlays of Kugler colors: gold-amber, ruby, white, dark red center line, on optic glass base with indentation, 5½ x 13 x 4¾

68. *Parallelograms,* 1980
Barium/potash glass with multiple cased overlays of Kugler colors: ruby, red-amber, gold-amber, beige, white center line, 4 x 4¾ x 2½ and 4½ x 4¼ x 2½

69. *Super Ellipse,* 1980
Barium/potash glass with multiple cased overlays of Kugler colors: ruby, peach, amber, red, red center line, white opal glass base, 6¾ x 8½ x 7¾

70. *Golden Squared Ellipsoid,* 1980
Barium/potash glass with multiple cased overlays of Kugler colors: gold-amber, red-amber, blue, opaque yellow, white center line, 5⅛ x 4½ x 6½

71. *45° Diagonal Rectangular Sections,* 1980
Barium/potash glass with multiple cased overlays of Kugler colors: white, ruby, red and blue, white center line, 6¼ x 12 x 2¼, 6¾ x 5 x 3, and 7 x 5¼ x 2

72. *Trapezoidal Form,* 1981
Barium/potash glass with multiple cased overlays of Kugler colors: yellow, orange, red, blue, white center line, 7½ x 11 x 5½

73. *Ovoid Prismatic,* 1981
Barium/potash glass with multiple cased overlays of Kugler colors: ruby, gold-amber, red-amber, beige, white, dark center line, 7½ x 7 x 8

74. *Ruby Twisted Column,* 1981
Barium/potash glass with multiple cased overlays of Kugler colors: ruby red, gold-amber, blue, beige, white center line, 16½ x 5 x 5

75. *Split Twisted Arc,* 1981
Barium/potash glass with multiple cased overlays of Kugler colors: gold-amber, red-amber, blue, white center line, 7 x 17 x 2

76. *275° Gold Amber Rotation,* 1981
Barium/potash glass with multiple cased overlays of Kugler colors: amber, thin lines over yellow, off-white, white center line, 18¼ x 5¼ x 5, and 4 x 8 x 4

77. *Yellow Discus Sectioned,* 1981
Barium/potash glass with multiple cased overlays of Kugler colors: yellow, ruby, darker ruby, steel blue, white center line, 3¾ x 5 x 10 each

78. *Curvilinear Sectioned Ovoid,* 1981
Barium/potash glass with multiple cased overlays of Kugler colors: red-amber, gold-amber, beige, alabaster, red center line, 5 x 16 x 3 each

79. *White Flat and 90° Twisted Vertical Arcs,* 1982
Barium/potash glass with multiple cased overlays of Kugler colors: alabaster, red with white lines, gold, blue, white center line, 15¼ x 22 x 10

80. *Extended Loop Form,* 1982
Barium/potash glass with multiple cased overlays of Kugler colors: blue, alabaster, yellow with colored lines, beige, white center line, 13½ x 20½ x 12

81. *Crossed Pile,* 1982
Barium/potash glass with multiple cased overlays of Kugler colors: blue, ruby with lines, yellow, white center line, 8 x 31 x 16

82. *Blue Twist,* 1982
Barium/potash glass with multiple cased overlays of Kugler colors: blue, ruby with lines, yellow amber, white center line, 20 x 16 x 4

83. *Blue Paired Arcs*, 1983
Barium/potash glass with multiple cased overlays of Kugler colors: blue, red with lines, yellowish white, white, white center line, 13 x 20 x 3 and 14 x 20 x 3

84. *Red Curvilinear Pair*, 1983
Barium/potash glass with multiple cased overlays of Kugler colors: thin veil of terracotta, ruby with lines, yellow, blue, white center line, 11¼ x 8 x 8 and 2 x 5 x 8

85. *Blue Crossed Form*, 1983
Barium/potash glass with multiple cased overlays of Kugler colors: blue, red with lines, yellow, alabaster, white center line, 12½ x 13 x 13

86. *120° Segment*, 1983
Cut and sandblasted optical lens blanks manufactured by Corning Glass Works, Danville, Virginia, and barium/potash glass with concentric cased overlays of Kugler colors: yellow, red-amber with lines, gold-amber, blue and red center line, 15½ x 20 x 17½

87. *Opalescent Red Crown*, 1983
Barium/potash glass with multiple cased overlays of Kugler colors: terracotta, ruby with lines, yellow, blue, white center line, ten pieces, 28 x 30 x 23

88. *75° Segment*, 1983
Cut and sandblasted optical lens blanks manufactured by Corning Glass Works, Danville, Virginia, and barium/potash glass with multiple cased overlays of Kugler colors: gold-amber, red-amber with lines, ruby, white, blue center line, 17 x 24 x 17½

89. *Penetrated Disc*, 1983
Sandblasted optical lens blanks manufactured by Corning Glass Works, Danville, Virginia, and barium/potash glass with multiple cased overlays of Kugler colors: ruby, gold-amber, yellow, blue center line, 17 x 45 x 17½

90. *Red Segmented Form*, 1983
Barium/potash glass with multiple cased overlays of Kugler colors: ruby, yellow with lines, amber, blue, white center line, 3½ x 23 x 14

91. *Terracotta Vertical Movement*, 1983
Barium/potash glass with multiple cased overlays of Kugler colors: terracotta, yellow with lines, red, blue, white center line, 22¼ x 24 x 15

92. *Opalescent Yellow Squared Descending Group*, 1983
Barium/potash glass with multiple cased overlays of Kugler colors: beige, yellow with orange lines, ruby, blue, red center line, 14 x 24 x 12

93. *Blue Counter-Balanced Form*, 1983
Barium/potash glass with multiple cased overlays of Kugler colors: blue, yellow with lines, ruby, orange, white center line, 11 x 15 x 7

94. *Juxtaposition*, 1983
Barium/potash glass with multiple cased overlays of Kugler colors: opal white, ruby with orange lines, yellow/beige, blue, white center line, 7½ x 20 x 16

95. *Red-Orange Pair*, 1983
Barium/potash glass with multiple cased overlays of Kugler colors: red, yellow with orange lines, red-amber, blue, white center line, 12½ x 12 x 14

96. *Red Interrupted Descending Form*, 1983
Barium/potash glass with multiple cased overlays of Kugler colors: ruby, yellow with orange lines, gold-amber, blue, white center line, 13½ x 14½ x 6

97. *Rose Opal Combination Arc*, 1983
Barium/potash glass with multiple cased overlays of Kugler colors: white, ruby with orange lines, yellow-beige, blue, white center line, 15½ x 17¼ x 3¼ as mobile arc, 18½ x 15 x 3¼ as vertical arc

98. *Yellow Crown*, 1983
Barium/potash glass with multiple cased overlays of Kugler colors: yellow, ruby with orange lines, blue, white, ruby center line, eleven pieces, 23 x 28 x 23

99. *Blue-Green Linked Forms*, 1983
Barium/potash glass with multiple cased overlays of Kugler colors: blue, yellow with orange lines, red, orange, white center line, 12½ x 18 x 18

100. *Orange Triple Movement,* 1983
Barium/potash glass with multiple cased overlays of Kugler colors: thin terracotta, yellow with orange lines, ruby, orange, white center line, 16 x 19 x 17

101. *Powder Blue Veiled Combination Arc,* 1983
Barium/potash glass with multiple cased overlays of Kugler colors: thin blue, yellow with orange lines, ruby, blue, white center line, 15 x 14 x 4½ and 6 x 7 x 2½

Prints from Glass Plates

102. *Trial I,* 1974
Intaglio print on Arches paper, 10¼ x 6½, edition of 50

103. *Trial II,* 1974
Intaglio print on Arches paper, 19 x 15¾, edition of 50

104. *Aurora,* 1974
Intaglio print on Arches paper, 10 x 17, edition of 50

105. *10° Rotation,* 1981
Suite of five intaglio prints on Arches paper, 18¼ x 16¾, edition of 50

106. *00 Buckshot,* 1983
Intaglio print from automobile safety glass plate shot with a shotgun, 20 x 15¾, edition of 20

107. *#6 Birdshot,* 1983
Intaglio print from automobile safety glass plate shot with a shotgun, 20 x 15¾, edition of 20

108. *Origami,* 1983
Suite of four intaglio prints on Arches paper, 19¾ x 15½, edition of 50

Selected Bibliography

Statements by Harvey Littleton in Books, Articles, and Conference Proceedings

"Artist Produced Glass: A Modern Revolution." *Studies in Glass History and Design.* Papers Read to Committee B Sessions of the VIIIth International Congress on Glass, Held in London, 1st-6th July 1968. Ed. R. J. Charleston, Wendy Evans, and A. E. Werner. Sheffield: Society of Glass Technology, 1970, 109-10. Reprinted from [*Czech*] *Glass Review,* 24, No. 7 (1969), 193-94.

"Gallé: Transcendence in Glass and Wood." *Craft Horizons.* 37 (Aug. 1977), 32-36, 67.

"Glass—A Potential for Printmaking." *Glass Art Society Journal,* 1982-83, 63-65.

Glass Art Society Newsletter, 3 (1978), 81. Reprinted in "Littleton's Furnace." *Glass Art Society Journal,* 1 (1979), 90.

"Glass by Erwin Eisch." *Craft Horizons,* 23 (May 1963), 14-17.

"Glass in the Ozarks." *Craft Horizons,* 33 (April 1973), 42, 57-58.

Glassblowing: A Search for Form. New York: Van Nostrand-Reinhold, 1971.

"Harvey K. Littleton." *Neues Glas,* Jan.-March 1983, 2.

"Littleton Remembers. . . ." *Glass Art,* 4, No. 1 (1976), 20-31.

"Media Discussion/Glass." *The Craftsman's World.* American Craftsmen's Council, 1959, 176.

New American Glass: Focus West Virginia, Part 1. Huntington, West Virginia: Huntington Galleries, 1976.

"A Potter's Experience with Glass." In *Research in the Crafts.* New York: American Craftsmen's Council, 1962, 42-44.

Proceedings of the Seventh National Sculpture Conference. Lawrence, Kansas: National Sculpture Center, 1972.

"Wisconsin Designer-Craftsmen." *Craft Horizons,* 19 (Jan. 1959), 42.

Films Featuring Harvey Littleton

Hot Glass. Milwaukee, Wisconsin, WMTV and the Milwaukee Art Center, 1967.

A Search for Form. Madison, Wisconsin, WHA-TV, with the American Crafts Council, 1973.

Books and Articles about Harvey Littleton

Anderson, Donald James. "Artists Are Blowing Bubbles That Last Almost Forever." *Chicago,* 9 (Nov./Dec. 1972), 25-27.

Atkinson, Tracy. "Harvey K. Littleton, Bergstrom Art Center." Review of *Harvey K. Littleton: A Search for Form* exhibition. *Glass Art,* No. 1 (1976), 47-48.

Beard, Geoffrey. *Modern Glass.* London: Studio Vista/Dutton, 1968.

Bruner, Louise. "Glass Workshop." *American Artist,* 33 (Feb. 1969), 48-53, 76-77.

Byrd, Joan Falconer. "Harvey Littleton—'The Core of Everything. . .Is the Work.'" *Arts Journal,* 4 (May 1979), 2-3. Also printed in *Glass Art Society Journal,* 1 (1979), 101-03.

Byrd, Joan Falconer. "Harvey Littleton: Pioneer in American Studio Glass." *American Craft,* 40 (Feb. 1980), 2-7.

Charleston, Robert J. *Masterpieces of Glass: A World History from the Corning Museum of Glass.* New York: Abrams, 1980.

Cohen, Robert A. "Origins of the Studio Glass Movement." *Glass Studio,* No. 32 (May 1982), 36-42, 51-54.

Colescott, Warrington W. "Harvey Littleton." *Craft Horizons,* 19 (Nov. 1959), 20-23.

Colescott, Warrington W. "Littleton Prints from Glass." *Craft Horizons,* 35 (June 1975), 28-29.

Conroy, Sarah Booth. "Borrowing from Modern Artists." *Washington Post,* 15 April 1979, Sec. E, 9.

Contemporary Studio Glass: An International Collection. Ed. National Museum of Modern Art, Kyoto. New York, Tokyo, Kyoto: Weatherhill/Tankosha, 1982.

DiNoto, Andrea. "New Masters of Glass." *Connoisseur,* 211 (Aug. 1982), 22-24.

Eidelberg, Martin. "Ceramics." In *Design in America: The Cranbrook Vision, 1925-1950.* New York: Abrams, 1983.

"The Family Tree of Glassblowing." *Glass Art,* 4, No. 1 (1976), 38-39.

"Glas Heute." *Artis,* 9 (Sept. 1972), 28-31.

"Glaspapst Harvey K. Littleton zum ersten Mal in einer europaischen Glasgalerie." Review of exhibition, Essener Glasgalerie, Essen. *Porzellan*

& Glas, No. 11 (1982), 31.

"Glass Comes Home to Penland." *Arts Journal*, 2 (June 1977), 6-8.

"Glass Sculpture." *Glass Industry*, 50, No. 5 (May 1969), 248-49.

Gould, Elizabeth. "Harvey Littleton." Review of exhibition, Madison Art Center, Wisconsin. *Craft Horizons*, 28 (July 1968), 33.

Grover, Ray and Lee. *Contemporary Art Glass*. New York: Crown, 1975.

Gundaker, Grey. "Harvey Littleton at Hunter Museum, Chattanooga." *ArtCraft Magazine*, 1, No. 1 (Dec. 1979/Jan. 1980), 77-78.

Gutcheon, Beth. "Frozen Motion." *New York Times Magazine*, 8 Feb. 1976, Sec. 6, 60-61. Reprinted with different illustrations as "In Frozen Motion." *Horizons USA*, No. 16, 44-49.

Hall, Julie. *Tradition and Change*. New York: Dutton, 1977.

Hammel, Lisa. "International Show on Esthetic of Glass." Review of *New Glass* exhibition, Metropolitan Museum of Art, New York. *New York Times*, 20 Nov. 1980, Sec. C, 6.

Hampson, Ferdinand. "New Interest in Glass Sends Prices Soaring." *Glass Art Society Journal*, 1981, 38-40.

Hartman, Marti. "Three Craftsmen in Glass." *Glass Art Magazine*, 3 (June 1975), 22.

"Harvey Littleton." *Cross-Country Craftsman*, 14 (Aug. 1963), 1, 4.

Higgins, Michael. "Show of Blown Glass at the Art Institute of Chicago." Review of *Harvey Littleton* exhibition. *Craft Horizons*, 23 (Sept. 1963), 43.

Hunter-Stiebel, Penelope. "Contemporary Art Glass: An Old Medium Gets a New Look." *Art News*, 80 (Summer 1981), 130-35.

Hunter-Stiebel, Penelope. "20th Century Decorative Arts." *Metropolitan Museum of Art Bulletin*, Winter 1979/80, 49.

In Praise of Hands: Contemporary Crafts of the World. Essay by Octavio Paz. Foreword by James S. Plaut. Toronto: McClelland and Stewart, 1974.

Jepson, Barbara. "Art and Antiques: Glorious Glass: Hot New Art Medium." *Town and Country*, 138, No. 5044 (Jan. 1984), 123-25.

Labino, Dominick. *Visual Art in Glass*. Dubuque, Iowa: William C. Brown, 1968.

Landay, Janet. "Erwin Eisch, Harvey Littleton." Review of exhibition, Habatat Galleries,

Lathrup Village, Michigan. *New Art Examiner*, 9, No. 1 (Oct. 1981), 21.

Melvin, Jean. *American Glass Paperweights and Their Makers*. Camden, New Jersey: Thomas Nelson, 1967.

Meredith, Dorothy. "Exhibiton at Milwaukee Art Center." Review of *Harvey Littleton: Glass* exhibition. *Craft Horizons*, 26 (March 1966), 40, 51.

Miro, Marsha. "Littleton: The Name in Art Glass." Review of *Harvey K. Littleton: Glass Sculpture* exhibition, Habatat Galleries, Dearborn, Michigan. *Detroit Free Press*, 5 March 1978, Sec. B, 11.

Moynehan, Barbara. "Glass Art Revived in Studio Movement." *New York-Pennsylvania Collector: Arts and Antiques*, 1 (June 1976), 2, 10.

Norden, Linda. "New York: American Craft Museum 25th Anniversary." Review of *Beyond Tradition* exhibition. *Craft International*, Winter 1982, 43-45.

Nordness, Lee. *Objects: USA*. New York: Viking, 1970.

"One Man Glass." *Country Life*, 145, No. 3752 (30 Jan. 1969), 240.

Pearson, Katherine. "Glass." *Horizon*, May 1979, 62-67.

Pearson, Katherine. *American Crafts: A Source Book for the Home*. Stewart, Tabori & Chang, 1983, 112-113, 114, 118.

Perrot, Paul. Review of *Glassblowing: A Search for Form*, by Harvey K. Littleton. *Craft Horizons*, 32 (June 1972), 10, 69-70.

Philippe, Joseph. "Cristalleries du Val Saint-Lambert: Créations et Pièces Uniques de Collignon (Liège, Belgique) et Littleton (U.S.A.)." *La Vie Liégeoise*, Dec. 1972, 3-14.

Philippe, Joseph. *Le Val Saint-Lambert*. Liège, Belgium: Librairie Halbert, 1974.

Reif, Rita. "A Museum's Contrast in Crafts." Review of *Objects: USA, the Johnson Collection* exhibition, Museum of Contemporary Crafts, New York. *New York Times*, 1 Oct. 1976, Sec. C, 17.

Review of *Glassblowing: A Search for Form*, by Harvey K. Littleton. *American Artist*, 36 (Sept. 1972), 66.

Review of *Littleton-Bailey* exhibition, St. Louis Artist-Craftsmen League, St. Louis, Missouri. *Craft Horizons*, 23 (July 1963), 41.

Ricke, Helmut. "Unikat und Serie, eine Orientierungshilfe." *Neues Glas*, No. 1 (April 1980), 13-17.

Slivka, Rose. "Littleton." *Britannica Encyclopedia of American Art*. Chicago: Encyclopedia Britannica Educational Corporation, 1974.

Smith, Dido. "Exhibition: Harvey Littleton." Review of *Harvey K. Littleton: Glass Sculpture* exhibition, Lee Nordness Galleries, New York. *Craft Horizons*, 30 (Dec. 1970), 60.

Smith, Dido. "Offhand Glass-Blowing." *Craft Horizons*, 24 (Jan. 1964), 23-23, 53-54.

Smith, Dido. Review of *Harvey K. Littleton: Glass Sculpture* exhibition, Lee Nordness Galleries, New York. *Craft Horizons*, 29 (May 1969), 54-55.

Weinstein, Joel. "A Conversation with Harvey Littleton." *Glass Art*, 1, No. 4 (Aug. 1973), 42-47.

Exhibition Catalogues Containing Comments by or about Harvey Littleton

Bloomfield Art Association. *National Glass*. Introduction by James K. Boatner. Birmingham, Michigan, 1971.

Corning Museum of Glass. *New Glass: A Worldwide Survey*. Corning, New York, 1979.

Detroit Artists Market. *Michigan Glass, 1980*. Juror's statement by Harvey K. Littleton. Detroit, 1980.

The Four Arts at Governor's Square and Florida State University. *Harvey K. Littleton*. "Littleton Glass: Mathematics and Invention" by Allys Palladino-Craig. "From the Studio" by Harvey K. Littleton. Tallahassee, 1983.

Heller Gallery. *Harvey K. Littleton: Glass Sculpture*. "Introduction: A Quest Rewarded: Harvey Littleton and the Studio Glass Movement" by Penelope Hunter-Stiebel. New York, 1982.

Jesse Besser Museum. *Glass: Artist and Influence*. Introduction by Eugene A. Jenneman. "Glass: Artist and Influence" by Ferdinand Hampson and Paul Hollister. Alpena, Michigan, 1981.

John Nelson Bergstrom Art Center. *Harvey K. Littleton: A Search for Form: 1946-1975*. Introduction by Anthony V. Garton. Neenah, Wisconsin, 1975.

Lee Nordness Galleries. *Harvey K. Littleton: Glass Sculpture*. Introduction by Tracy Atkinson. New York, 1970.

Milwaukee Art Center. *Harvey Littleton: Glass*. Introduction by Tracy Atkinson. Milwaukee, 1966.

Mint Museum of Art. *Harvey Littleton*. Introduction by Paul J. Smith. Charlotte, North Carolina, 1979.

Museum of Contemporary Art. *American Crafts '76: An Aesthetic View*. Introduction by Bernard Kester. Chicago, 1976.

Museum of Fine Arts. *Contemporary Blown Glass by Southeastern Artists*. Introduction by Joan Falconer Byrd. St. Petersburg, Florida, 1982.

Toledo Museum of Art. *Toledo Glass National*. Introduction by Otto Wittmann. Toledo, Ohio, 1966.

Toledo Museum of Art. *Toledo Glass National II*. Introduction by Otto Wittmann. Toledo, Ohio, 1968.

Toledo Museum of Art. *Toledo Glass National III*. Introduction by Otto Wittmann. Toledo, Ohio, 1970.

Toledo Museum of Art. *American Glass Now*. Introduction by Otto Wittmann. Toledo, Ohio, 1972.

University of Kansas. *Twenty-fifth Annual Kansas Designer-Craftsman Exhibition*. "The Contemporary Craft Scene" by Harvey K. Littleton. Lawrence, Kansas, 1980.

University of Wisconsin-Oshkosh. *The Wisconsin Movement—Glass in Form*. Introduction by Joan Falconer Byrd. Oshkosh, Wisconsin, 1982.

Western Carolina University. *Erwin Eisch Retrospective: Glass and Drawings*. Introduction by Harvey K. Littleton. Cullowhee, North Carolina, 1980.

Western Carolina University. *North Carolina Glass '76*. Introduction by Harvey K. Littleton. Cullowhee, North Carolina, 1976.

Western Carolina University. *N. C. Glass '78*. "How Cheap Technique" by Thomas S. Buechner. Cullowhee, North Carolina, 1978. Includes a statement by Harvey Littleton.

Western Carolina University. *North Carolina Glass '80*. Cullowhee, North Carolina, 1980. Includes a statement by Harvey Littleton.

Western Carolina University. *North Carolina Glass '82: Invitational Exhibition*. Cullowhee, North Carolina, 1982. Includes a statement by Harvey Littleton.

Collections

Addison Gallery of American Art, Andover, Massachusetts

American Craft Museum of the American Craft Council, New York City

Arnot Art Museum, Elmira, New York

Australian Council for the Arts

Birmingham Museum of Art, Birmingham, Alabama

Birks Museum, Milliken University, Decatur, Illinois

Charles H. MacNider Museum, Mason City, Iowa

Chrysler Museum, Norfolk, Virginia

City Art Museum of St. Louis, Missouri

Cooper-Hewitt Museum, New York City

Corning Museum of Glass, Corning, New York

Decorative Arts Museum, Prague, Czechoslovakia

Decorative Arts Museum, Vienna, Austria

Detroit Institute of Arts, Detroit, Michigan

Detroit Children's Museum, Detroit, Michigan

Duke University Hospital, Durham, North Carolina

Elvehjem Museum of Art, University of Wisconsin, Madison, Wisconsin

Everson Museum of Art, Syracuse, New York

Fine Arts Museum of the South, Mobile, Alabama

Glasmuseum, Frauenau, West Germany

Glasmuseum, Wertheim a.M., West Germany

Greenville County Museum of Art, Greenville, South Carolina

Groningen Museum, Groningen, Holland

Handwerkskammer, Cologne, West Germany

Handwerkskammer, Munich, West Germany

Hastings College, Hastings, Nebraska

High Museum of Art, Atlanta, Georgia

Hokkaido Museum of Modern Art, Sapporo, Japan

Huntington Galleries, Huntington, West Virginia

Illinois State University, Normal, Illinois

Indiana University of Art Museum, Bloomington, Indiana

J. B. Speed Art Museum, Louisville, Kentucky

John Nelson Bergstrom Art Center and Mahler Glass Museum, Neenah, Wisconsin

Jones Gallery of Glass & Ceramics, East Baldwin, Maine

J. Patrick Lannon Foundation, Palm Beach, Florida

Kestner Museum, Hanover, West Germany

Krannert Art Museum, University of Illinois, Urbana, Illinois

Kunstgewerbe Museum, West Berlin, East Germany

Kunstgewerbe Museum, Cologne, West Germany

Kunstmuseum, Düsseldorf, West Germany

Kunstmuseum, Veste Coburg, Coburg, West Germany

Leigh Yawkey Woodson Art Museum, Wausau, Wisconsin

Madison Art Center, Madison, Wisconsin

Memorial Union, University of Wisconsin, Madison, Wisconsin

Memphis Brooks Museum of Art, Memphis, Tennessee

Metropolitan Museum of Art, New York City

Milwaukee Art Museum, Milwaukee, Wisconsin

Morris Museum of Arts and Sciences, Convent, New Jersey

Museum Bellerive, Zurich, Switzerland

Museum Boymans, Rotterdam, Holland

Museum für Kunsthandwerk, Frankfurt a.M., West Germany

Museum of Art, Albion College, Albion, Michigan

Museum of Fine Arts, Houston, Texas

Museum of Glass, Liège, Belgium

Museum of Modern Art, Kyoto, Japan

Museum of Modern Art, New York City

Museum Stuttgart, Stuttgart, West Germany

National Glass Museum, Leerdam, Holland

National Museum of American Art, Smithsonian Institution, Washington, D.C.

Northern Illinois University, Dekalb, Illinois

Ohio State University, Arthur E. Baggs Memorial Library, Columbus, Ohio

Oklahoma Art Center, Oklahoma City, Oklahoma

Prairie School, Racine, Wisconsin

Rahr Civic Center and Museum, Manitowoc, Wisconsin

Republic of San Marino

R. J. Reynolds Corporation, Winston-Salem, North Carolina

Ross C. Purdy Museum of Ceramics, Columbus, Ohio

S. C. Johnson and Son, Inc., Racine, Wisconsin

Sheldon Memorial Art Gallery, Frank M. Hall Collection, University of Nebraska, Lincoln, Nebraska

St. Paul Gallery and School of Art, St. Paul, Minnesota
Toledo Federation of Art Societies, Toledo, Ohio
Toledo Museum of Art, Toledo, Ohio
University Art Collection, Matthews Center, Arizona State University, Tempe, Arizona
University of Michigan Museum of Art, Ann Arbor, Michigan
University of Wisconsin Center, Wisconsin Rapids, Wisconsin
Utah State University, Logan, Utah
Victoria and Albert Museum, London, England
Western Illinois University, Macomb, Illinois
Wichita Art Museum, Wichita, Kansas

Photograph Credits
Corning Museum of Glass: catalogue nos. 1, 18
John Littleton: catalogue nos. 3, 5-14, 16, 17, 19-25, 27, 28, 30-36, 38-41, 43-46, 48-55, 57-59, 61-81
Diane Ralston: page 19
Smithsonian Institution: catalogue no. 26
Brian Westveer: front cover, inside cover, pages 10, 11, 25, 107; catalogue nos. 2, 4, 15, 29, 37, 42, 47, 56, 60, 82-101

Colophon
This book was typeset and printed by National Graphics, Inc. of Decatur, Georgia, in an edition of 500 hardbound and 3500 softbound copies. The text is set in Goudy Bold Roman and Goudy Old Style Roman and Italic.